CONSTELLATIONS

Like the future itself, the imaginative possibilities of science fiction are limitless. And the very development of cinema is inextricably linked to the genre, which, from the earliest depictions of space travel and the robots of silent cinema to the immersive 3D wonders of contemporary blockbusters, has continually pushed at the boundaries. **Constellations** provides a unique opportunity for writers to share their passion for science fiction cinema in a book-length format, each title devoted to a significant film from the genre. Writers place their chosen film in a variety of contexts – generic, institutional, social, historical – enabling **Constellations** to map the terrain of science fiction cinema from the past to the present... and the future.

'This stunning, sharp series of books fills a real need for authoritative, compact studies of key science fiction films. Written in a direct and accessible style by some of the top critics in the field, brilliantly designed, lavishly illustrated and set in a very modern typeface that really shows off the text to best advantage, the volumes in the **Constellations** series promise to set the standard for SF film studies in the 21st century.'
Wheeler Winston Dixon, Ryan Professor of Film Studies, University of Nebraska

 facebook Constellations

Constelbooks

T0324438

CONSTELLATIONS

ROBOCOP

Omar Ahmed

Omar Ahmed

is a UK-based film scholar, specialising in Indian cinema, and the author of *Studying Indian Cinema* (Auteur, 2015). He is currently completing a PhD at the University of Manchester.

Acknowledgements

The author would like to thank John Atkinson at Auteur for his kind and generous support in letting me write this monograph on a favourite film from my youth. Much of this monograph was a weekend job, squeezed in between teaching commitments and PhD research, and written in the musty corridors of the Manchester University Library. I would also like to thank Tom Dixon at Aquinas College with whom I spent many memorable years teaching film, my mentor and friend Rajinder Dudrah, my brother Faisal and writers James Clarke and Josh Hurtado for their encouragement.

First published in 2018 by
Auteur, 24 Hartwell Crescent, Leighton Buzzard LU7 1NP
www.auteur.co.uk
Copyright © Auteur 2018

Series design: Nikki Hamlett at Cassels Design
Set by Cassels Design www.casselsdesign.co.uk
Printed and bound in Great Britain

British Library Cataloguing-in-Publication Data
A catalogue record for this book is available from the British Library

ISBN paperback: 978-1-911325-25-3
ISBN ebook: 978-1-911325-26-0

Contents

Dedication

For Jubilee Home Video, Old Street – my local VHS haunt when I was growing up in Ashton-Under-Lyne in the 1980s and early 90s.

Key Credits and Synopsis

Key Credits

Director: Paul Verhoeven
Writers: Edward Neumeier, Michael Miner
Starring: Peter Weller, Nancy Allen, Ronny Cox, Kurtwood Smith, Miguel Ferrer
Producer: Jon Davison
Cinematography: Jost Vacano
Editing: Frank J. Urioste
Music: Basil Poledouris
Casting: Sally Dennison, Julie Selzer
Production Design: William Sandell
Art Direction: John Marshall, Gayle Simon
Costume Design: Erica Edell Phillips
Special Makeup effects: Rob Bottin
Distributor: Orion Pictures
Release dates: US – July 17, 1987; UK – February 5, 1988
Running time: 103 minutes

Synopsis

In a dystopian future, Detroit is a city ridden with crime and on the verge of collapse. A mega corporation, Omni Consumer Products (OCP), has taken control of the Detroit police force and plans to implement a new program to bring crime under control. After police officer Alex Murphy (Peter Weller) is massacred while on duty, he is chosen by OCP to be the first volunteer for the RoboCop program. Murphy is transformed into a man-machine, a cyborg super-cop. But OCP's attempt to erase the memory of Murphy proves to be unsuccessful. In turn, RoboCop undergoes an existential crisis, leading to a search to reclaim his true identity and exact revenge upon the heinous perpetrators of his violent death.

Introduction

If fantasy is given to metaphor, it is also an open terrain which permits the deployment of more metonymic rhetorical forms. Indeed, it is in the future fantasy genre that one finds some of the most radical critiques of American society during this period. (Ryan & Kellner, 1988: 244)

Ghost(s) in the Machine

If one were to compile a canon of great science fiction films the inclusion of *RoboCop* would be problematic simply because of the puerile title. 'It's a film about a robotic cop!' the likely protest goes, leading to a facetious dismissal of its critical worth. A silly title[1] can be a hindrance if you want your film to be taken seriously. Science fiction and horror are two films genres that can suffer from such an affliction. While film titles are in some cases appropriately valid for the content, it is nonetheless a barrier when it comes to the art of canonising films. When director Paul Verhoeven first read the script to *RoboCop* it was the inane title which initially put him off the project. Similar science fiction films that feature cyborgs such as *The Terminator* (1984)[2] submerged in outlandish imaginings, call for a markedly acute suspension of disbelief. Given the way films are inevitably marketed, made palatable for audiences naturally means film titles are transformed to suit commercial inclinations often conflicting with the content of a film. In terms of high concept cinema, the title *RoboCop* is a moribund simplification of the film's existential core. Yet it is such outward simplicity that fosters a contradiction often lurking in Hollywood genre films like *RoboCop*.

RoboCop is a film from my youth. It was one of the first 18 certificate films I saw, illegally on VHS, along with *Predator* (1987, imprinting the image of Carl Weather's decapitated arm firing a machine gun hypnotically in slow motion) and *Rambo First Blood: Part II* (1985 – the exploding dart = exploding man had made me in adolescent rapture). *RoboCop* made me realise the only way to navigate the tumultuous vestiges of high school was to act out the best bits of 'hard body' action films, not discounting the endlessly repeatable 'let off some steam' quip in *Commando* (1985), which was deployed vigorously in many high school filmic discussions. None of this helped with being accepted though. It only made me seem more ridiculous. I soon found out that anyone who had seen the film furtively acted out the robotic moves in the safety of their bedroom while perfecting super-villain Clarence Boddicker's endlessly quotable 'Can you fly, Bobby?' with the right level of villainous disparage. Miraculously, Bobby is able to fly, but only onto the hood of a moving Detroit police car, manned by Officers Alex Murphy (Paul Weller) and Ellen Lewis (Nancy Allen) valiantly pursuing Boddicker and his supercilious goons. Imitating something we love is not exclusively a childhood predilection. Simulacra are an abundant technological exuberance, materialising continually in the film's narrative. For example, the infantile gesture of imitating screen images also vexes Murphy who replicates the gun twirling T.J. Lazer for his son's ephemeral pleasures. In fact, Murphy's transformation into RoboCop acts out the subconscious fantasy of T.J. Lazer in the most grotesque modus, through death, rendering the act of simulation altogether ghostly and pronounced.

Fig 1. Boddicker and Bobby in Van

RoboCop's reputation was an early source of ridicule, such was the fate of many violent films of the 1980s when sanitised by the puritanism of the BBC or ITV. It was a film that played several times on ITV, who butchered and cannibalised the epoch of my cinematic youth, thoughtlessly redacting swearing with less colourful language. Strangely enough, such unhelpful dubbing created an unintentional comic value that instructively told me Verhoeven's films were really absurdist comedies. ITV and the BBC did this on a constant basis, tampering with authorial intent, so that one harboured a special resentment for the way affective genre cinema was reduced to puritanical cultural debris. Indeed, the most notorious dubbing,[3] or should I say drubbing, takes place when RoboCop confronts an irate criminal robbing a liquor store. An endless loop of innate 'fuck you' replaced with 'why me?' produces an altogether unimagined philosophical spin on a moment of unfathomable rage. I guess the joy of viewing dubbed films was uncovering those pleasurable contradictions that shaped your enjoyment. Even worse to contemplate is that if *RoboCop* had failed at the box office it would have suffered the fate of being deemed a 'video nasty',[4] lost to the historical vacuum of discordant moral panics. While *RoboCop*'s influence is evident in the Hollywood action film genre, ideologically inert films such as Marvel's *Iron Man*[5] franchise lack the wit, grit and visceral touch of a mischievous auteur as Verhoeven.[6]

Fortuitously, the critical standing of *RoboCop* has grown over the years, in no small part aided by the intervention of Criterion, a specialist home video label, which was first to re-release the film on Laserdisc and then later on DVD in an unrated directors cut. While the Criterion edition of *RoboCop* has long been out of print, the film's inclusion in the Criterion library accentuates its merit as a seminal science fiction film; a key American work of the 1980s, overturning familiar genre trappings while its erudite philosophical address transforms the iconic Frankenstein narrative into an altogether more radical, theological work.

Going Home[7]

Having opined on the personal, cinephile value of *RoboCop*, before I go further with chapter details I want to begin with a short analysis of a sequence from the film.

In science fiction cinema technological machines habitually regain or gain self-consciousness, taking on a life of their own. When repressed memories return they do so with an urgency that leads to a traumatic re-imagining of the past. Such a theme seems almost critical to science fiction films involving cyborgs, the fusion of man and machine begetting a cataclysmic identity crisis: 'The cyborg's status is neither human nor artificial but a hybrid of the two, radically altering human subjectivity' (Springer, 1996: 33). In 1987 such a proposition may have appeared to be another cinematic prophecy ruminating on our interminable technological enslavement yet writer Donna Haraway's 'A Cyborg Manifesto' (1984) had already argued such fantasy was in truth a reality:

> By the late twentieth century, our time, a mythic time, we are all chimeras, theorized and fabricated hybrids of machine and organism: in short, we are all cyborgs. The cyborg is our ontology; it gives us our politics. (Haraway, 1985: 191)

Haraway's words were indeed timely. Such a prophecy did come to pass. We now occupy a reality that sees us transfixed with technology. Claudia Springer says 'techno-eroticism', a feature of cyberpunk culture, with antecedents in early twentieth century, is 'the passionate celebration of technological objects of desire' (Springer, 1996: 3) linking technology and sexuality into a dystopian bind. Our bodies have become wedded to phones, tablets and laptops in such a personal way that we are constructs of our own virtual worlds; transient souls, ghosts in the machine.

Omni Consumer Products' (OCP) attempt to erase the original identity of Murphy fails spectacularly, triggering an existential crisis that seems almost perpetual today, leading to the poignant 'going home' sequence. When RoboCop, empowered with the truth about his past, returns to his home, surveying the now empty spaces, recalling fragments of a familial past you would be mistaken you were watching a science fiction film. The sequence begins with RoboCop in his patrol car, surveying a suburban neighbourhood. The open, clean spaces of 'Primrose Lane' cues us into the past imagined as a nostalgic utopia, a stark contrast to the wretched spaces of inner-city Detroit. Urban inaptness may recall Fritz Lang's *Metropolis* (1927) but it is one of the rare occasions in the film when we get to see Detroit as a city divided on not solely economic but class lines, which is explored largely through the attacks on corporate power. RoboCop's entrance to the house is greeted by a video recording of a virtual estate agent on a TV monitor. As RoboCop makes his way through the house, the use of non-diegetic music, Basil Poledouris'[8] haunting score, frames the rekindling of memories as both distressing and purgative.

The first of three brief flashbacks in this sequence recalls a memory of his son watching T.J. Lazer on TV, a science fiction Western. When his enthused son turns to his father asking, 'Can you do that Dad?' the first of many POV shots are used to exchange Murphy for RoboCop, juxtaposing past and present, emotionalising the identity crisis. Murphy's physical absence from the flashbacks, which are cleverly substituted with a POV approach, gives the sequence an auxiliary ghostliness. This sequence also poses a deeper theological question about the meaning of the soul or inner self. Although Murphy no longer exists and is biologically dead, his memories are tied to his soul,[9] which remains very much alive. As RoboCop continues through the house, his agitated state is exacerbated by the irritating sales pitch of the virtual estate agent, a reminder of a corporate capitalist world of which he is now a public servant.

Fig 2. Polaroid of Family

Next, RoboCop comes across a charred photograph of his wife and son, initiating the second flashback. This flashback unfolds in the kitchen during Halloween and sees the family pose for a self-portrait (a polaroid selfie). Again RoboCop enters the ghostly space through the POV of Murphy, reminding us of the family he once had. The deep sense of loss reaches its conclusion in the third and final flashback when he moves into the bedroom, recalling the memories of his wife telling Murphy she loves him. Regaining the consciousness of a ruptured identity corporatised by OCP while left for dead by the dregs of Detroit, RoboCop's self-loathing reaches an impasse. He lashes out, punching the TV monitor still playing the video of the indifferent estate agent, smashing the ephemeral and eviscerating his technological self. He sees a paradise lost, a life that he will never be able to return to or retrieve, as his place within society is altogether consumable. The ferocity of the punch, read ideologically, denotes the resentment RoboCop harbours towards corporate omniscience, intruding on the personal, in this case his memories.

However, an alternate psychological reading of this sequence insinuates a gendered facet in which RoboCop's discovery of his identity as Murphy reintroduces a 'masculinity in crisis' theme first evident in the opening of the film. As he ventures through the empty house RoboCop realises his role as father and husband have been shattered. Since he is both man and machine, this potentially escalates the masculinity in crisis to something much broader about his non-gendered state and what Springer has termed 'bodily obsolescence' (Springer, 1996: 24). RoboCop's realisation of his impotency, since he will never be able to love or have sex, is registered metonymically when he punches the TV monitor, a phallic gesture, transitorily purging a self-loathing, reminding us 'the cyborg is a creature in a postgender world' (Haraway, 1984: 192). As this sequence testifies, the film may transcend but it is also tied to the science fiction form in the outer sense. In terms of iconography, classic science fiction tropes are patent, and *RoboCop* functions viscerally as a superior genre film.

Chapter Summaries

The first chapter will map out the film's broad genre positioning, engaging with stylistic, thematic and narrative virtues of the Western film genre and reading the film's genre markers as oppositional. The gangster and Western film genres are interchangeable, arguably the only difference being visual iconography. The urban crime thriller, an adjunct of the gangster film, is present in much of *RoboCop*'s genre design. Nonetheless, it is not hard to see it as a hybrid text, fusing together elements from science fiction, horror, action and the Western.[10] Christine Cornea (2007) says science fiction rests between horror and the musical, arguing all three rely on the spectacle. While the film most clearly occupies the cyborg sub-genre, intertextual nods (*High Noon* – 1952, *Shane* – 1953) to the Western genre calls for a closer re-reading of the film to determine its porous genre status. Readings of *RoboCop* have remained static, fixed on its relationship with obvious genre markers but a clearer genre re-interpretation in terms of the Western film points to its richness as a pluralistic genre text. The dialogue, the villains, the final showdown are all imported from the Western yet the film's ability to draw on conventional visual and narrative ideas of the Western also include broader thematic qualities intrinsic to the ideological fabric of the Hollywood Western such as justice, civilisation, social order and morality, many of which are reciprocal with the gangster/crime genre.

In his seminal discussion of *RoboCop* as a postmodern text, Steve Best (1989) talks of the 'technification of the body' in relation to commodification. Both themes, intertwined, are very much by-products of corporations claiming our bodies through labour, technology and the promulgation of false needs. Murphy's transformation into a product by OCP establishes a master and slave dialectic made problematic by the man-machine equation. Most pertinently, his memories become OCP property. The science fiction genre in the 1980s regularly portrayed corporations and the unchecked power they wielded as detrimental to the proletariat worker.[11] This brief cycle of films including *RoboCop*, *Outland* (1981) and *Aliens* (1986) depicts the corporation as a pathological entity. In the case of *RoboCop*, the proletariat cyborg regains his self-consciousness, resists temporarily but stops short of putting an end to neo-fascist corporatisation. RoboCop has a complicated relationship with OCP and unlike a radical science fiction anti-hero such as Ripley (Sigourney Weaver) in the *Alien* films who defies the corporatisation of her body (referring here in particular to the much-maligned *Alien 3* [1992]), RoboCop believes in the restoration of social order, framing the film in ambiguous ideological terms, recalling producer Jon Davison's remarks, who labelled the film as 'fascism for liberals'. When finally in the boardroom at the end, RoboCop reinforces the status quo, saving 'the old man' (an indexical Ronald Reagan), preserving an on-going capitalist corporate hegemony. In the context of corporatisation, most tangible is the way Murphy's body is technified, fetishised, commodified and corporatised to perform a specific ideological function, forming a major part of this chapter's discourse.

Juxtaposed to the cartoonish violence of *RoboCop* is a satirical edge, lampooning Reagan's neoliberal America. The anarchic fun in the film's script is amplified by the involvement of Paul Verhoeven. Satire, a key approach, would also form a central part of examining fascism in *Starship Troopers* (1997), the final film in Verhoeven's dissident Hollywood science fiction trilogy, also including *Total Recall* (1990). In *RoboCop*, a target for ideological critique is the mainstream American media, specifically the news channels and ad breaks, forming a parallel narrative. Verhoeven ridicules Reagan's toxic American culture industry mixing fear, dumbing down and propaganda to win consent from the people. The film may have been set in the future but in many ways the politics are of the now. Concurrently to the media as a source of mockery are public issues such as a police force which has been corporatised, a direct result of neo market liberalism, and now faced with strikes, an exponential crime rate and increasing number of police officers killed in the line of duty. Old Detroit's 'cancer of crime' we discover is fuelled by corporate greed, another neoliberal value, epitomised in the figure of corrupt corporate villain Dick Jones (Ronny Cox) who is part of the same nexus of crime he has been assigned to eradicate. The construction of a new Detroit, 'Delta City', also raises the question of gentrification, another consequence of neoliberalism that was felt across many of the major cities in Reagan's America. Ironically, the apocalyptic vision of Detroit,[12] 'Detropia', that *RoboCop* presents has come to fruition, with a city in apparently terminal decline. The middle ground RoboCop takes up, negotiating between public and private interests, emphasises the film's ideological ambivalence towards accountability in both spheres.

Director Paul Verhoeven's fascination with Christ appears through ocular images in many of his films. Verhoeven tried but failed to make a film on Christ in the 1990s, but that did not stop him from writing a book on the subject, published in 2011 under the title *Jesus of Nazareth*. Interpreting *RoboCop* as a Christian allegory explains the cult status of the film, as it continues to be open to broader philosophical debate. *RoboCop* as an American Jesus holds credence if one considers the populist narrative of Christ is visible in the imagery of martyrdom, resurrection, and death that permeates the film. Verhoeven has even remarked that RoboCop walks on water, performing a miracle. Murphy returns to the people of old Detroit as a kind of saviour,

Fig 3. Verhoeven on set of the film

a neo-fascist messiah figure, intervening directly in the crimes perpetrated against the innocent but at the behest of a new religion, the world of corporate capitalism. Prophets that can be created take the shape of cyborgs now. A theoretical intersection here is the work of Donna Haraway's 'A Cyborg Manifesto', offering a new gendered reading of the film, with a consideration of Officer Lewis, Murphy's streetwise partner.

RoboCop was Paul Verhoeven's first American film. Although *RoboCop*'s status as a key science fiction is now secure, on its release American film critics were divided in their opinions, fixating on Verhoeven's love of violence. In fact, the critical reception of *RoboCop* was markedly different in Europe with critics in the UK embracing the film's subversive qualities. Interestingly, a pattern emerges in the 1980s in regards to edgy, unconventional science fiction films like *Blade Runner* (1982) which were given a rough ride in comparison to softer, mainstream science fiction cinema like *E.T.* (1982). Some of this negative criticism can be explained in relation to the low cultural standing of science fiction as a film genre, not taken seriously as other seemingly more respectable genres. It will be significant to revisit the initial reviews and re-contextualise the critical responses, considering ideological bias, genre readings, Verhoeven's authorial status, and other notable factors. *RoboCop* is also part of a trilogy of science fiction films directed by Verhoeven, including *Total Recall* and *Starship Troopers*, both of which develop further ideological interests about American culture. Positioning *RoboCop* within this trilogy and formulating textual and thematic links between the three films will also offer further insights into the film's connectedness with Verhoeven as an auteur. Finally, *RoboCop* spawned a number of sequels, a TV show, video game and other media, establishing itself as an unlikely franchise. Most recently, *RoboCop* has been reworked for a new audience and the film's influence can be detected in many science fiction films, including *Chappie* (2015).

It's almost impossible that a film as dark, twisted and destabilising as *RoboCop* would come out of Hollywood today. One wonders how exactly the film slipped through the net. Perhaps more surprising was the film's unexpected success at the box office, emerging as a sleeper hit for Orion Pictures. Certain aspects of the film's visual design have dated, clarified in terms of budgetary reasons, but the film's ideological machinations are germane as ever. *RoboCop* remains a key text in the cyborg cyberpunk sub-genre, evincing the way genres are vehicles for ideological and authorial subversion. This monograph will contribute to the growing discourse on contemporary science fiction cinema, exploring *RoboCop* from a series of new critical approaches while enriching existing ones.

Chapter I: Genre Mutations

In *Screening Space* (1997) Sobchack talks of the tyranny of genre categorisation:

> Definitions strive, after all, for exclusivity, for the setting of strict and precise limits which, when they become too narrow, seem glaringly and disappointingly arbitrary. (Sobchack, 1997: 17)

Applied to *RoboCop*, and many genre films, we risk creating essentialist doctrines, unreasoned approaches leading to conservative interpretations of texts, consolidating the mythical immutability of dominant cinema. The infantile binary opposition between good (art cinema) and bad cinema (the mainstream) still persists, and it is veiled by the interminably varying discourses of global cinephilia in which audience pleasures are also prematurely, naively debated and ultimately repressed in the pursuit of intellectualism. There has and continues to be the cloak of respectability that some film genres strive to manifest; the fear that mainstream, populist acceptance signals a monolithic entombing, that visceral pleasures have to be theorised and in many cases dismissed in the face of ideological contexts. While a film like *RoboCop* has been intellectualised in the interdisciplinary fields of technology, Reaganomics, cyborg politics and science fiction, an alternate genre reading will posit *RoboCop* retains pluralistic pleasures connected to historiographies of American imaginings, recalling the unconscious semantics of the Western.

In this first section I will present a reading of *RoboCop* as a Western. Though the film's hybridity has been mentioned especially in regards to science fiction's interrelatedness with horror, and in the intertextual nods to *Shane* (the gun twirling signature of Murphy/RoboCop), it has not been explored at length to sufficiently argue for iconographic slippages that account for the salience of the Western. My intention with this reading is not to argue for the re-categorisation of *RoboCop* as a Western. Such a rationale cannot be broadly sustained. But to widen the possibilities of looking intimately at the way iconographic details can create genre dissonance, what is known as vraisemblance: 'the correspondence of a text to some cultural model which already accepted as natural and understood' (Lane, 1985: 180).

This reignites two key sites of contestation: firstly, that all films are in fact super-texts seemingly impossible to categorise, and secondly, reductionist categorisation of texts obfuscates and simplifies thematic, aesthetic complexities. Furthermore, reframing genre readings means retracing the intersections with the horror (Barry Keith Grant's work on the Yuppie Horror film) and science fiction. This includes accommodating for developments such as the science fiction Western, a sub-genre that has veered from innovation (*Westworld*, 1973) to derision (*Wild Wild West*, 1999) yet continues to elicit new rejoinders (*Cowboys and Aliens*, 2011; *John Carter*, 2012).

Since the 1970s the work of influential film scholars have tried to contest the uniform discourse of the Western film genre. Briefly outlining some of this work will be significant to the analytical approach. It was Bazin who in 1955 coined the term 'superwestern', which he deemed to be an evolution of the Western genre specific to the post war era:

> The superwestern is a western that would be ashamed to be just itself, and looks for some additional interest to justify its existence – an aesthetic, sociological, moral, psychological, political or erotic interest, in short some quality extrinsic to the genre and which is supposed to enrich it. (Bazin, 1955: 151)

The 'superwestern' was most pronounced in the work of Anthony Mann, Budd Boetticher and Delmer Daves. And the mixing of genres produced some remarkable sub-genres such as the Noir Western, resulting in films like *Pursued* (1947), *Ramrod* (1947) and *The Ox-Bow Incident* (1943).

Robert Warshow (1962) delineated the key characteristics of the genre, namely the criticality of heroism, guns and violence as a foundational preoccupation. The first wave of scholarly discourse utilised structuralism to determine narrative. William Everson (1969) presented one of the first comprehensive studies of the Western film genre, isolating a common narrative and thematic language. Focusing on the mechanics of plots that form the basis of narratives in most Westerns, Everson identified twelve groups, which he argued were repeated invariably. Structuralism sought to reduce the Western to a set of patterns that sometimes denied the existence of hybridity. Wright (1975), like Everson, emphasised narrative commonalities, as did Jack Nachbar (1974). Both Everson and Wright borrowed from Northrop Frye's five modes 'defined in terms of the range and power of action of the

Fig 4. The Superwestern; Shane *and* Pursued.

protagonist' (Pye, 1975: 240) including Myth, Romance, High Mimetic Mode, Low Mimetic Mode and The Ironic Mode. Douglas Pye (1975) also relatedly discusses Frye's work but with a marked interest in the romantic narrative.

The introduction of the auteur theory to film studies in the 1960s saw a marginal shift away from structuralism. The work of Jim Kitses (1970) sought to examine the tensions between authorial traits and genre conventions. John Cawelti (1975) took a completely alternate perspective of the Western, looking at the theme of violence and its relationship to wider sociological and psychological assumptions in American culture. By the 1970s the Western had met its demise but there was still an incongruent cycle of films, mainly revisionist, released by Hollywood. This led to a redress of scholarly work. Beginning with Philip French (1977), his tenacious reexamination of the genre led to an acute ideological analysis considering the way the Western had started to digress, while Tag Gallagher[13] (1986) also intervened, disputing the long held claims the Western evolved with a linearity that mirrored changes in American society. Recent studies of the Western such as Neil Campbell (2013) elucidate the transgressive nature of the genre, accounting for the way the dormant nature of the Western produces intermittent cycles of films with an altogether unconventional perspective. Although I have tried to summarise some of the scholarly work that interests this project it is only a snapshot of what is an eclectically robust discourse.

When Philip French says 'there is no theme you cannot examine in terms of the western, no situation which cannot be transposed to the West' (French, 1977: 23) he enunciates the malleability of the form, which has over the decades accommodated for multifarious themes. Since *RoboCop* is a hybrid work, the competing genre signifiers mask Western idioms. I want to focus mainly on the opening sequences including Murphy's arrival at the precinct but the analysis will inevitably open out, locating iconographic markers of the Western film, and referring to isolated moments in the film's narrative that substantiate some of the genre slippages.

The Frontier

The first idea to address is the opening shot; a sweeping and unnerving aerial shot, moving across the Detroit River, and stopping at the nocturnal, anonymous city skyline. This is juxtaposed to the film's title appearing sensationally in the middle of the frame to the discordant steely music of Basil Poledouris, establishing the dystopian urban milieu of Detroit. While the conventionality of this establishing shot adheres to classical Hollywood narrative, its ordinariness recalling dominant American crime imagery fetishises the city space, educing the iconography of mountainous landscapes to loosely denote the frontier in the Western genre. The film uses the urban skyline to signify the frontier, framing Old Detroit as the untamed West, a hostile, 'wild' space in which law and order has spiralled out of control, oppositional to Delta City as a new civilisation. Pye argues 'the life of the frontier was both ennobling because it was close to nature, and primitive, at the farthest remove from civilization' (Pye, 1975: 145). The disconnect here is that we are in the future, although how far into the future is deliberately never made explicit, so in terms of American history, the frontier no longer exists. Carter writes, 'by the late nineteenth century, the wilderness as the index of American social 'reality' was being replaced by the industrial cities' (Carter, 2014: 30). Reframed in the context of dystopian science fiction cinema, the city is a regressive space; a spectral wilderness has returned in the symbolic reality of Old Detroit. Steve Neale describes the frontier as 'the meeting point between Anglo-Americans and their culture and nature and the culture of others' (Neale, 2000: 134) and while this cannot be strictly applied to

Fig 5. Delta City

RoboCop, Old Detroit's symbolic status as the Old West represents a geographical boundary for corporate expansionism by OCP. However, worryingly, the ideological symbolism of Old Detroit becomes lost in the revenge narrative, a point of contention which I will return to later in terms of the film's problematic ideological address.

Conventionally, the creation of RoboCop, establishes the imperative to tame the wilderness so it can be 'made safe for settlement' or in this case corporate colonisation (and gentrification) in the vision of Delta City, a Utopian project which aims to regenerate civilisation. Old Detroit works doubly as a 'contested space' (Schatz, 1981: 83) in which 'forces of social order and anarchy are locked in an epic and unending struggle' (ibid.), epitomised moralistically in the base conflict between RoboCop, the gunfighter, and Clarence Boddicker, the unruly villain. Returning to the opening sequence, as the city is announced, the narrative segues into the first media break which aside from satirising our mortality, a classic moral equation of law and order, often found in the most basic of Western film narratives, is firmly established through the news report describing the anarchy of Old Detroit. The report details a nightmarish wilderness in which the partial massacre of police officers perpetrated by 'the unofficial crime boss of Old Detroit' Clarence Boddicker has led to union leaders censuring OCP for their failure to manage the police department.

Monolithic binary oppositions dictating the traditional structure of Western narratives has been theorised by Kitses as 'series of antimonies' that point to a 'shifting ideological play' (Kitses, 1970: 11) such as savagery vs. humanity which 'are at the heart of ideas about the West (Pye, 1975: 48). Boddicker is framed in such terms as the lawless bandit/outlaw, depicted in an unflattering monochrome image, creating a mythical aura of monstrosity around his villainous character while falsely establishing him as the source of anarchy in Old Detroit. Equivalently, the introduction of Boddicker proposes someone will need to civilise the West, looking forward to Officer Alex Murphy.

In many Westerns the disappearance of the frontier not only meant the obliteration of the cowboy from the new urban landscapes but progress was routinely demarcated as inevitable in the flow of history. In *RoboCop* the promise of progress that Delta City yields is another Western idiom elucidating the greed of capitalist growth and conquest. The idea of progress is exemplified in the speech given by the 'Old Man', the corporate head of OCP to the board of executives:

> In six months we begin construction of Delta City where Old Detroit now stands. Old Detroit has a cancer. The cancer is crime and it must be cut out before we employ the two million workers that will revive this city. Shifts in the tax structure have created an economy ideal for corporate growth. But community services, in this case, law enforcement have suffered. I think it's time we gave something back.

The triptych of the Old Man, Dick Jones and Clarence Boddicker admittedly omits the culpability of Bob Morton, the surrogate father of RoboCop, but it is a corporate alignment that serves to complicate the true source of villainy. Interestingly, Dick Jones' manipulation of Boddicker for his own capitalist gain recalls the fatalistic alliance between Morton and Frank in Leone's *Once Upon a Time in the West* (1968), another film about progress, history and capitalism. In the Old Man's speech, the problematic of crime described as a 'cancer', something that is incurable, is altogether more explicit in the intertextual linkages to the Western's imaginings of township.

The dream of Delta City espoused by the Old Man relates to what Philip French says about the way the Western has been appropriated over time by a 'much larger international set of attitudes and beliefs' (French, 1977: 22), one of them being 'the need for American politicians to define their public posture in relation to national mythology' (ibid.), a trait associated with Reagan's presidency, and subsequent Republican presidencies including Bush Snr. and Jnr. in which the imagery of the cowboy, a marker of provincial masculinity, re-entered national media discourses. *RoboCop* scriptwriter Edward Neumeier has said the Old Man is a deliberate allusion to Ronald Reagan yet the film opts for an unusually benign representation.

The introduction of ED-209[14] as the future of law enforcement can also be equated to Western narratives involving the contest over land rights that regularly saw cattle barons, corrupted symbols of capitalism, hiring outlaws to kill trespassers and illegal immigrants, as captured so vividly in Michael Cimino's *Heaven's Gate* (1980).[15] While we could draw parallels between the way OCP deploys robots to expunge the 'cancer of crime' to the way mercenaries and outlaws were paid to protect the interests of capitalism in the Old West, the introduction of RoboCop, a hybrid of man and machine, complicates this narrative disposition as he is still a servant of OCP, even up until the final moments of the film.

Murphy the Westerner

The conventions of the Western are even more pronounced in Murphy's introduction. This sequence begins with an establishing shot of the exterior to 'POLICE PRECINCT, METRO WEST'. We then cut to inside the precinct and interrupt a sleazy lawyer protesting to Sergeant Reed (Robert DoQui)[16] that a supposedly misplaced attempted murder charge against his unsavoury client should be downgraded to assault. Reed listens apathetically, labelling both the lawyer and client 'scumbags', ejecting them from the police station. The Western iconography of the saloon and jailhouse is conflated and reimagined in the setting of the police station with Reed functioning as the Sheriff. A departure from the whiteness of the American Western is reversed by the presence of a black Sergeant that offers a link to the racial diversity of Detroit. It was not uncommon in Westerns set in a town that narrative action typically revolved around a central meeting place such as the saloon. The chaotic *mise-en-scène* of the saloon is visible in the transparency of the police station, populated by the dregs of Detroit while Reed struggles to maintain law and order, an action that constantly preoccupies the Sheriff. By having Reed refuse the advances of the lawyer signifies both his authority as an honest blue collar lawman and establishes the power he exercises over the precinct, an aspect of his hard-edged personality, which will later collide with the indifference of OCP.

Murphy's entrance is not signposted in the traditional star[17] context usually given to the iconic figure of the cowboy/gunfighter. Here it is deliberately understated, laconically so, as Murphy's ordinariness serves to confound audience expectations when he is killed later on. One aspect of Murphy's entrance, if contextualised in the idioms of the Western, which does remain relatively stable, is his status as an outsider, a tension that quickly dissipates once Murphy teams up with his partner. The casting of Peter Weller is critical here since his laconic, toned physique and sunken cheekbones are classical visual traits of the cowboy. (It is a shame no one ever cast Weller in an actual Western, as it is a natural milieu for him). Murphy's status as an outsider is hailed to us when he approaches the front desk, saying he has been transferred from Metro South, 'a nice precinct', only to be undercut by Reed's somewhat self righteous reality check: 'We work for a living down here, Murphy.' Murphy is taken aback by the veiled class politics of Reed and although it momentarily creates separateness, it accentuates his label as an outsider, recalling once again Western conventions.

After Murphy is introduced to his colleagues, interrupted by the announcement of Officer Frank Frederickson's death, he returns to the front desk. This time the conflated iconography of the saloon and jailhouse is made altogether explicit. This is achieved through inverting the anarchic and seedy milieu of the saloon, typically denoted as a masculine domain, with the introduction of a female officer, disrupting homogenous conceptions of this gendered space. In fact, Raymond Bellour (1993) says the Western film cannot function without the presence of the woman. If so, what position does Lewis occupy? Is she decorative, intrinsic or subjugated? Expanding on Bellour's point about the centrality of women to the very fabric of the Western, Cawelti argues women were 'primarily symbols of civilization' (Cawelti, 1975: 47). This is true in many respects especially in films that sees the cultured woman from the city

Fig 6 & 7. Murphy twirling his gun, Lewis chewing gum

encountering the depravity of the wilderness and in some cases helping to civilise even the cowboy.

While one could argue Lewis is underwritten and appears tokenistic at times, her introduction, much more dynamic and overstated than Murphy's, in fact sets her up as a hero. The disempowerment of Murphy establishes a dynamic that runs contrary to the gender conservatism of the Western. Cawelti argues that although 'the presence of women invariably threatens the primacy of the masculine group' (Cawelti, 1975: 63), which is certainly not the case with *RoboCop*, 'the woman in effect takes over the role of the masculine comrades and becomes the hero's true companion' (ibid.). Here a correlation persists in Lewis's role as arbitrator, coming between the wilderness and civilisation, acting as RoboCop's 'true companion' but also negotiating an alternate female identity. The first impression Lewis makes on Murphy is also significant, recalling male bonding in Western films (see the work of Howard Hawks)[18] that often see men/women complementing each other on their physical attributes and skills, something which Murphy does after Lewis disarms her unruly suspect. 'Partnering up' is an idiom of the detective genre in which an unlikely bond between two strangers can often provide a major source of dramatic conflict or humour, as is the case with the Buddy film. A similar notion is at work in *RoboCop*, one that is unconventionally represented since Murphy and Lewis's relationship is devoid of antagonism.

The Post-Western

So far I have tried to consider sequences from the film framing narrative actions and genre conventions as invocations of the Western. I want to broaden this line of enquiry by arguing *RoboCop* can also be labelled as a post-Western. Neil Campbell characterises post-Western films as 'generically impure' and 'transgressive' that permit 'relation, reflection and critical interaction' (Campbell, 2013: 24) with the rest of the genre. Philip French is more specific in how the post-Western can be defined, offering linkages to *RoboCop*'s often acknowledged intertexts to *Shane*:

> ...central to them all is the way in which characters are influenced by, or are victims of, the cowboy cult; they intensify and play on the audience's feelings about, and knowledge of, Western Movies. (French, 1977: 140)

'The cowboy cult' that French points to can be located in *RoboCop*. It is important to note French talks of 'the cowboy cult' in the context of the post-Western, films made in the late 1960s and 1970s, such as Peckinpah's *The Wild Bunch* (1969). French frames this idea in destructive terms, arguing mythology blinds people to reality, just as cinema can. Imagery of the cowboy as a mythical entity has been absorbed into American popular culture and is manifested in *RoboCop* through the simulacra of T. J. Lazer, which is an argument I will explore next. Prior to Murphy and Lewis's encounter with Boddicker and his goons, they pause for a coffee. The exchange of words, centring on Murphy's gun twirling spectacle is worth looking at further:

Lewis: Pretty fancy moves, Murphy.
Murphy: Yeah, well, my son Jimmy watches this cop show, T. J. Lazer. This Lazer does this when he takes down a bad guy. So my kid thinks a good cop...
Lewis: And you don't wanna disappoint him.
Murphy: Yeah, well, role models can be very important to a boy.
[A pause as Lewis looks at Murphy.]
Murphy: OK, OK, I get a kick out of it.

Murphy's signature gun-twirling indicative of supposedly formidable gunplay, or simply postmodern mimicry, is a central motif in the film's narrative. It is a ghostly memory, connecting the past and present, and has its antecedents in the imagery of the Westerner. This acute motif chimes with French's argument that characters in the post-Western are 'influenced by, or are victims of, the cowboy cult' (French, 1977: 140), a point supported by Kuenz's discussion of *RoboCop* in relation to Owen Wister's 1902 novel 'The Virginian', a template for the early Western film genre:

The figure of the cowboy continues to serve in the United States as the definitive type of masculine heroism in the face of normalizing conventions. (Kuenz, 2001: 99)

Murphy claims he does not want to disappoint his son, replicating a stoic, parochial construction of fatherhood. But he is also a victim of false masculine identities perpetuated by the media that in turn cannibalises popular imagery such as the Western. This induces a problematic in terms of a hyper-reality that will come undone in Murphy's encounter with Boddicker, codified in the overstated ultimatums of the westerner. 'Dead or Alive, you're coming with me!,'[19] exclaims Murphy when he first confronts Emile, an unsavoury thug. Lewis and Murphy's brief yet substantial exchange about 'his fancy moves' articulates a universal fear that fathers harbour about disappointing their sons, hinting at Murphy's anxieties concerning his own masculinity. This is taken to its lucid nightmarish extremes when Murphy is resurrected as RoboCop, a hyper masculine imitation of T. J. Lazer, and role model for the children of Detroit.

The fleeting presence of Jimmy, Murphy's son, as a link to the symbolic role of children in the Western is an important one.[20] French, argues children perform a 'triple role' in the Western:

> ...being trained to take their place in society; being caught up in, and possibly corrupted by, the western myth and the mystique of Frontier violence; reminding us that the aggressive instinct and a fascination with violence are things we are born with. (French, 1977: 75)

French speaks of a pact between violence, constructions of masculinity, and the positioning of children as a natural process. In the case of Jimmy, one can see how 'the western myth' and 'fascination with violence' are normalised and naturalised in a fictional show like T.J. Lazer and later in Morton's imagining of the cowboy cult as RoboCop. Later in the film when RoboCop visits his home, a flashback, recalling the image of Jimmy watching T.J. Lazer, shows the young boy mesmerised by the spectacle of gunplay. Campbell's discussion of *Shane*, supportive of French's position, and read in relation to Murphy and Jimmy's connection is demonstrative of this thematic bind of children, violence and the Western:

> Shane may well bring death with him in the form of the six-gun, and Joey might be too young for the moment, but the hard fact is that, from the very outset, the child is actually being culturally indoctrinated, as it were, for a masculine social trajectory with violence at its core. (French, 1977: 58)

However, Murphy is also corrupted by the mythology of the West as he falsely imagines and conflates his status as a cop with that of a cowboy, one who can heroically take on the bad guys and win. If language and intertextual linkages demarcate the Western genre, the film also recalls classical Western framing, codifying the film further. One of the first instances of Murphy's gunplay is depicted in an asymmetrical low angle composition in which Murphy's larger than life juxtaposition to the Detroit cityscapes reproduces the conventional image of the Westerner as both powerful and mythical. Murphy's gunplay may seem impressive at first, but it is undermined in the prior sequence in which Morton declares the RoboCop program is ready to start 'as soon as some poor schmuck volunteers'. While Morton's contempt for the people of Detroit resonates of a corporate Yuppie arrogance it also reminds us of the dangers of Murphy's romantic preoccupations with being a cop. Central to the gun twirling motif are two other salient points, intrinsic to the Western genre: violence and gunplay, both of which will later become defining features of RoboCop's superiority.

The influential work of John Cawelti is relevant here. Cawelti has discussed the Western as a projection of the myths of violence fundamental to American culture, masculinity and the story of the West. Violence is paramount to Verhoeven's science fiction work and while it is a trait attributed to authorial concerns Cawelti argues, 'in the Western, violence is characteristically the hero's means of resolving the conflict generated by his adversary' (Cawelti, 1975: 24). The historical relationship with violence and guns characteristic of many American genres including the gangster and noir comes directly out of the Western, one fraught by complications:

> The interaction of American attitudes towards violence and the image of Western hero as gunfighter is so complex that it seems impossible to determine which causes the other. (Cawelti, 1975: 57)

RoboCop, a gunfighter reimagined by corporate America is based on the morally dubious void that some situations can only be resolved by violence is an argument Cawelti posits for the Western: 'the American tradition has always emphasized individual masculine force' (Cawelti, 1975: 58). A cycle of hard body action films (see Jeffords 1994) made in the 1980s including *Rambo First Blood: Part II* inscribed Reagan's interventionist, imperialist foreign policy onto the hyper-masculine bodies of Sylvester Stallone and Arnold Schwarzenegger. In *RoboCop*, arguably a hard body film, 'expression of masculine potency' is communicated by both Dick Jones and Bob Morton in their mechanical, technological creations. RoboCop and ED-209 replicate the traditional Western means of 'the six-gun' (Cawelti, 1975: 58) in a more militarised, anarchical form. Debatably, *RoboCop* is a work that fetishises guns, problematic in light of the ongoing gun control dispute in America. This is an aspect of the film that has been overstated in terms of the militarisation of Reagan's America in the 1980s.

However, by resituating the argument of guns in the realms of Western iconography, traditions and history, reasons that a film's genre intertexts can sometimes be downplayed at the expense of over contextualising ideological determinants.

Genre Vagaries: Horror

A consideration of Western themes, notably the savage, the massacre and revenge, intersecting with the horror genre, form the next part of this chapter. After failing to apprehend Boddicker and his band of motley outlaws, Murphy and Lewis track Boddicker to an abandoned steel mill in which they are hiding out. This leads to the violent massacring of Murphy. Before discussing the sequence closely, I want to briefly consider the way Boddicker and his gang are framed in terms of the Western genre.

The derelict steel mill, iconic of a collapsed Detroit industry, becomes a no man's land, hostile territory (yet another Western idiom) so to speak, in which Murphy and Lewis are subjected to lawlessness. Cawelti says, 'the second major character role in the Western is that of the savage. The savage symbolizes the violence, brutality and ignorance which civilized society seeks to control and eliminate...' (Cawelti, 1975: 52). In the past, the savage was the Native American, the marauding Red Indian, a monolithic and troubling racist representation gradually contested and ultimately revised in the 1960s and 1970s. In *RoboCop*, the savage and outlaw are brought together symbolically in Boddicker's venal characterisation as one of many complicated manifestations of villainy:

> ...one of the major organizing principles of the Western is to so characterize the villains that the hero is both intellectually and emotionally justified in destroying them. (Cawelti, 1975: 14)

Such moral justification is staged as a horrific spectacle in the massacre and death of Murphy. Before Murphy's capture, Lewis and Murphy decide not to wait for backup, carrying on with their dangerous pursuit. While it is Lewis and Murphy's duty as police officers to apprehend Boddicker, Murphy's arrogance, interpreted as a form of idealism, extending from his imaginings as a cowboy, recalls a sense of chivalry that can be traced as far back as *The Virginian* (1902). Furthermore, since Murphy is new to the precinct and has yet to prove his worth as a cop, he doubly sees the opportunity to apprehend Boddicker as a way of satisfying an anxious masculinity linked to his role as a father. While the scenario of the cowboy or gunfighter outgunned by a band of outlaws is a fairly generic convention of the Western, the imagery of the massacre, often associated with marauding Native Americans savaging a group of white settlers, intersects with the horror genre, producing the first of many 'epic moments' (Cawelti, 1975: 36) in the film.

The massacre is a spectacle iconographic of many genres including the gangster film but its centrality to the Western can form a major source of narrative disruption. For example, in *The Searchers* (1956), the massacre of Ethan Edwards' (John Wayne) extended family, establishes the central goal of retrieving Lucy (Natalie Wood), Edwards' niece, who has been kidnapped by the Indians. The massacre initiates the epic search, which forms the narrative arc of the film, sending Ethan and Martin (Jeffrey Hunter), on a hero's quest. George Lucas would pay homage to *The Searchers* massacre sequence in *Star Wars: A New Hope* (1977), an innovative, hypnotic blend of science fiction and the Western tropes.[21] Both of these examples and many others testify to the historical materiality of the massacre as suggestive of an imperialistic horror but also a marker of savagery.

Paul Verhoeven reads Murphy's death as crucifixion, a religious ideological interpretation that I will explore in depth later. But the frissons with Christianity also intersect with the Western since the Puritanical settlers, civilising the wilderness with the importation of religious doctrine, uncertainly frames Boddicker and his outlaws as the savage Indians. The blonde haired, blue-eyed family man that is Murphy clearly represents the sort of Puritanical saviour often identified in the masculine heroism of Western mythology.

Returning to the massacre, Murphy enters the steelworks and is quickly apprehended by Boddicker's henchmen who surround him. Boddicker interjects, claiming he wants to be the one to kill Murphy. This happens in parallel to Lewis's temporary subjugation by Joe, the tokenistic African American hoodlum in Boddicker's mob, which occurs in a characteristically sardonic moment of sexual curiosity. When Murphy and Boddicker

Fig 8. The massacre of Murphy

first meet, Verhoeven frames them in a symmetrical medium two shot, the top part of their bodies filling the frame in almost equal proportions. Such classical framing recalls the Western genre, a staging device used to saliently delineate the conventional oppositions between hero and villain. But the symmetry in the shot, suggesting both characters have something in common, points to the complicated, interchangeable role of Murphy, since his reincarnation as RoboCop, will see him timidly question his role as a public servant. Next, Boddicker jokingly removes Murphy's helmet and puts it on Emile. In doing so Boddicker begins to deconstruct Murphy, literally stripping away his identity as a cop, taunting him: 'You gotta be some kind of great cop, come in here all by yourself!' This pantomime of humiliation Murphy is made to endure not only feeds into the popular revenge narrative of the Western in which 'a hero seeks revenge against an outlaw or Indian who has wronged him' (Cawelti, 1975: 46) but synthesises comedy, horror and tragedy into an unnerving, contentious melange.

As the sequence unfolds, the unflinching horrors of the Western are clarified in the exhibition of violence, which begins with an act of bodily dismemberment. When Boddicker uses a shotgun to dismember Murphy's hand, a sharp cut to a near overhead shot pauses to to graphically depict the violence. Admittedly, the Western was very responsive in detailing the psychological impact of violence but due to censorship, especially in the 1940s, the physical impact of violence only really became a feature of the genre in the late 1950s and early 1960s. Determinants such as America's involvement in Vietnam run parallel with the meditations of masculinity and violence intrinsic to the semi-revisionist universe of Sam Peckinpah. In many ways, for the gunfighter in the Old West, the hands were the most precious commodity, expressing power, strength and creativity, and in this context, the physical annihilation of Murphy's gun hand becomes a symbolic destruction of his masculinity. This moment of sadism re-presents Boddicker as something more than just a criminal, or outlaw, creating an aura of horror that one can equate with the pathological, homicidal tendencies of the Monster in the horror film. Everything Detroit has tried to repress rises to the surface with Boddicker's nightmarish violence. Robin Wood writes:

> ...one might say that the true subject of the horror genre is the struggle for recognition of all that our civilization represses or oppresses, its reemergence dramatized, as in our nightmares, as an on object of horror, a matter of terror, and the happy ending (when it exists) typically signifying the restoration of repression. (Wood, 1982: 28)

Wood's idea of horror as a site of repression[22] overlaps with Barry Keith Grant's work on 'The Yuppie Horror Film' (1996). *RoboCop* does not directly fall under this cycle, but it certainly manifests frissons of Yuppiedom, most explicitly in Bob Morton. Grant's work identifies a denial amongst critics against the plurality of lower genres, arguing 'most critics who are concerned with genre theory or interested in the range of formal film categories deny that the genres of horror and science fiction are particularly flexible and adaptable' (Grant, 1996: 4). Denial is easily disproven; just simply consider the innovative sub-genres spawned by horror and science fiction – most pertinently, the zombie film. Grant defines a Yuppie as someone who: 'resides in or near one of the major cities, claims to be between 25 and 45, lives on aspirations of glory, prestige, recognition, fame, social status, power, money' (Grant, 1996: 5). Based on this criterion, is Murphy a Yuppie, although he is a police officer? The flashbacks certainly suggest Murphy has a relatively comfortably family lifestyle, is moderately affluent, and lives in a good neighbourhood, but whether or not this construction points to a Yuppie status is questionable. In truth, the real Yuppies are the OCP executives and Morton fits the criterion perfectly.

Grant talks of 'the descent by middle class characters into the hell of the inner city' (Grant, 1996: 6), which is certainly what happens to Murphy. However, unlike the middle class characters Grant talks of who are in a momentary crisis, when Murphy is reimagined as RoboCop, this becomes permanent, leading to the metaphorical loss of Yuppiedom. Furthermore, Grant also talks of the way Yuppie Horror films deploy the iconographic element of the 'old dark house' and 'making them into gothic, horrifying workspaces or living spaces' (ibid.). This is somewhat evident when RoboCop visits his house in the going home sequence, projecting the space as sterile, haunted and ghostly. In fact, this sequence, as discussed in the introduction, is the emotional heart of the film. The tragedy of Murphy is extrapolated here with a melancholy that chimes with the opinion of Cawelti: 'Of all the popular action-adventure formulas, the Western is the one which sometimes comes closest to tragedy' (Cawelti, 1975: 56).

A final idea Grant proposes ties in with traditional horror theory, that of the 'presence of the monster', and that in Yuppie Horror films 'the villains are commonly coded as such' (Grant, 1996: 7).[23] This is complicated since the monster from a creationist perspective is RoboCop but the villains are clearly perceptible and in this case strongly affiliated with corporate power. Boddicker is a monster; smart yet heinous. Grant develops the argument of villains, saying 'the evil characters in Yuppie horror movies function as the Other, as an external, disavowed projection of something repressed or denied within the individual psyche or collective culture' (Grant, 1996: 8). This applies to Boddicker more than anyone else. He is the doppelgänger of Dick Jones, of corporations, the darker, violent and pathological side of the corporation that is repressed in the public sphere. While not all of the conventions Grant theorises apply to *RoboCop*, it has shades of them, which again points to the film's porous nature as a genre text.

Having been tortured by Boddicker, Murphy gets to his feet, holding the bloody stump which was once his hand, turning to face the indiscriminate onslaught of Boddicker's goons who pummel Murphy's body with a barrage of gunshots.[24] Boddicker is a shadow of Dick Jones so it is doubly ironic that Murphy will be resurrected by OCP, the 'return of the repressed' (Wood, 1982), haunting his perpetrators like some unimaginable spectral entity. At the same time, the gunning down of Murphy, who imagines himself as the chivalrous cowboy, reiterates imagery of the wilderness often attributed to the Western, uncovering lawlessness, which will need resolving and dually establishing the classic revenge mission of the wronged hero. As I have previously stated, once Murphy is murdered, his resurrection as RoboCop sees the film shift into a more explicit science fiction context. But before I finish my re-reading of the film as a Western, I want to offer a brief discussion of two other sequences in the film that directly recall Western conventions and concluding with a consideration of *RoboCop* as an example of the Science Fiction Western.

The first of these sequences is RoboCop's microcosmical journey through the crime-infested streets of Detroit. Unlike Murphy's low-key entrance, RoboCop's introduction is orchestrated as a romantic, enigmatic spectacle. This starts with his arrival at the precinct, provoking curiosity amongst the police officers that scramble to get a glimpse of RoboCop, unofficially unveiled to the public in a moment of self-aggrandisement by Morton. As RoboCop strides out of the precinct, he catches the keys to the patrol car he has just been assigned. This showy gesture recalls an assuredness often evident in the repertoire of the swaggering cowboy,[25] and made altogether explicit in RoboCop's ferocious, precise gunplay, first witnessed by the precinct in yet another exhibition of Morton's arrogance. Peculiarly, Murphy's imaginings of T.J. Lazer comes to pass in a twisted technological aberration. He becomes the cowboy his son wants, but a spectral one.

The extended montage of RoboCop patrolling the city is constructed as an advertisement for a new kind of law enforcement, and since RoboCop is a product in the eyes of OCP, the montage establishes RoboCop as a brand – the city's heroic saviour, a messiah, who has descended upon the filthy streets just like the Sheriff assigned to enforce law and order in a disreputable frontier town. By thwarting a robbery, rape and hostage situation, three seemingly unrelated incidents, RoboCop is framed as if he was in on the joke, helping to promote OCP's new product as a solution to the 'cancer of crime'. Repeated low angle shots are used to represent RoboCop as a colossus, mythical spectacle of wonder, recalling conventional science fiction imagery of the 'Other' while also pointing to his potential monstrosity. But in

Fig 9. RoboCop patrolling the streets of Detroit

this complicated narrative address is a populist convention of the Western, romantic notions of the crusading lawman. Such romanticism is immediate once RoboCop leaves the precinct. Once in the patrol car, the vehicle is fetishised, including a close up of a headlight as it comes on and tyres burning rubber. Both are deeply clichéd images recalling in fact the urban crime film but it is not ridiculous to make the leap, translating the car as symbolic of the horse.

And as RoboCop drives through the streets, the musical score surges, the anvil clanging mimetically, celebrating the birth of this new soldier, and reiterating the primal idea of the chivalrous, gallant knight in armour going to do battle. This is the film at its most Hollywood, reinstating the loss of masculinity incurred by Murphy in a triumphalist instant of hard-body politics. In fact, all three of the situations that RoboCop comes across in this sequence are derivatives of stock narrative setups common to the Western but also to the urban crime genre. Firstly, we have the guy holding up the liquor store. One can find equivalence to the bank robber of the Western film narrative. Next, the intervention in a rape, not only affirms RoboCop's chivalry, but it is a situation not uncommon to stereotypically reductive gender norms of the Western genre in which a defenceless woman is rescued by heroic explications. However, awareness of such traditions is inverted when RoboCop shoots the rapist in the groin, pointing to a satirical affectation that is complemented by a robotic awkwardness. The final situation sees RoboCop disarming a city councilman who is holding the Mayor hostage. All three situations are filtered through a satirical prism, mocking the generic nature of American mainstream cinema and its reliance on formulaic narrative storytelling devices.

The Epic Moment

The final sequence to briefly explore is the ending, another of Cawelti's 'epic moments'. This begins with Murphy/RoboCop entering the corporate boardroom, presenting evidence of Dick Jones' complicity in the murder of Bob Morton. In a final act of desperation, Jones takes the Old Man hostage, refusing to turn himself in. Since the fourth directive prevents RoboCop from arresting any senior OCP officer, the Old Man fires Jones, thus releasing him from such immunity. RoboCop retorts with a polite 'thank you' and shoots Jones repeatedly. The impact of the gunfire makes Jones lose balance and he is thrown out of the window, falling to his bloody death. Calm returns to the boardroom, and as the Old Man straightens his tie, recovering from the ordeal unscathed, he turns to RoboCop who has just finished re-holstering his gun in celebration. 'Nice shootin', son! What's your name?' enquires the Old Man to which RoboCop replies emphatically 'Murphy', before walking away. Cue end titles.

The final confrontation with Dick Jones lacks the physicality of RoboCop's previous encounter with Boddicker since that is charged with a personal sense of revenge. But the apprehension of Jones brings closure to the film's narrative threads as RoboCop avenges the murder of Bob Morton. Although in this respect RoboCop is fulfilling his job as a police officer, implementing the directives, he is naively unaware of the complicity of Bob Morton's role in 'restructuring the police department with prime candidates', which led to Murphy's reassignment to a new precinct. Morton is just as much to blame for the death of Murphy, an argument that I will explore in a later chapter in terms of the film's complicated ideological address.

The gunning down of Jones is a classic yet simplistic image of the Western tradition; the bad guy going down in a hail of bullets. But the space in which the gunfight takes place, the boardroom, momentarily places RoboCop in the private, corporate sphere, a space that has previously witnessed a technological glitch, resulting in the death of 'Kinney', a corporate newbie. Since Jones uses corporate identity, power and immunity to evade public accountability, this makes the choice of the boardroom ideologically symbolic. And while this sacred corporate space is violated on many occasions, like the saloon, it is protected by RoboCop, a lawman, returning to Schatz's argument in which the 'westerner is motivated to further the cause of civilization by his own personal code of honour' (Schatz, 1981: 57). In other words, Delta City as a projection of the frontier is a Utopian fantasy upheld as a bizarre form of manifest destiny.

The Old Man is clearly impressed with RoboCop's gunplay, which he praises. Once again, in the Western, the ability to handle a gun was one of the ways in a man was judged in society, and the Old Man, symbolic of Reagan who often invoked the mythical West in his political rhetoric, sanctions RoboCop's violence, endorsing his masculine prowess and celebrating an 'individualist heroism' (Simmon, 2003: 124), reinforced through the language of the Western: 'Nice shootin', son!'. When RoboCop responds with 'Murphy', the reclamation of an identity erased and suppressed by OCP is a political statement, reconnecting with the individuality that characterised the cowboy in the Western. The laconic, minimal assertion of this identity is juxtaposed to the logo of OCP on the TV screens behind him. But this time the sea of red against which the logo is placed signifies the perpetual corrupt corporate world, which has blood on its hands, reiterating the permanency of RoboCop's enslavement. His commodification as a product means he will never be free.

Although he reclaims his identity and walks away, RoboCop is still the property of OCP, and thus in a way Murphy can only exist spectrally. As RoboCop says 'Murphy', the end credits commence, beginning with the title, 'ROBOCOP'. The placement of the title ROBOCOP immediately after the reclamation of MURPHY also reiterates an existential crisis remains, that he is both an insider and outsider, returning to a wider question about the social positioning of the police officer, as someone who moves freely between the public and private sphere but in the end belongs to neither.

Fig 10. RoboCop in the boardroom

Nonetheless, another reading of the film's ending in the context of Westerns such as *Shane*, demonstrates RoboCop freeing himself from the enslavement of OCP, and that his walking away at the end recalls the endings of many classic Westerns in which the cowboy, gunfighter or lawman has to depart because his masculinity is defined by a moral code of personal integrity and anonymity. Bazin says Shane is 'a pathfinder, who straddles the divide between civilization and savagery, between law and outlaw, between painful historical abstractions and utopian desires for the future American democracy' (Bazin, 1955: 50) and we can just easily say this about RoboCop's mercurial 'pathfinder' position especially in regards to the final sequences.

Redemption as a theme emerges in relation to the ending especially if we consider what Cawelti says about *Shane*:

> In *Shane*, the hero's return to his role as heroic gunfighter is clearly represented as an act of revitalization and redemption in which, through an act of violence, the hero saves the captive homesteaders and becomes one with himself. (Cawelti, 1975: 539)

While this is not as clear-cut in the ending to *RoboCop*, it does chime notably after RoboCop has been massacred a second time, this time by his own colleagues at the behest of Dick Jones. It is Lewis who helps him to revitalise so he can clearly find redemption, manifested in multiple acts of violence. There is undeniably a catharsis here at work when RoboCop shoots Jones, says his name and walks away, which is brought to a triumphalist crystallisation through the musical score that rises from the soundtrack over the end credits. In terms of audience pleasures, and in the context of the Western, the shootout is a cathartic paradigm, and there are no doubts that the pre-revisionist Westerns and other American film genres use closure as a site of reconciling narrative demands with audience expectations, something which *RoboCop* does with a brazen, unashamed elation.

In this chapter I have tried to re-read *RoboCop* as a Western, accounting for other genre intersections such as horror. I want to end with a brief note on *RoboCop*'s status and how it is categorised in the discourse of film journalism and academia. While I have stayed away from the hybrid term 'Science Fiction Western' in this reading, I have done so because *RoboCop* is not labelled consensually as such by writers, critics and scholars. Perhaps one of the reasons for this refusal to label *RoboCop* a science fiction Western rather than a dystopian science fiction action film is to do with the disrepute of the latter.

While it is evident a body of Science Fiction Western films do exist including *Westworld, Back to the Future Part III* (1990), *Wild Wild West, Cowboys and Aliens* to name a few, the sub-genre is often the subject of ridicule by critics and audiences. I'm not wholly convinced by the term either and I can see why *RoboCop* has thankfully not become a victim to such an arbitrary, unsatisfactory method of categorisation. *Star Wars: A New Hope*, a film that clearly pays homage to the Western, resides in the realms of fantasy and science fiction, not the Science Fiction Western sub-genre, because it draws on so many visible and invisible myths, genres and styles, a kind of cultural bricolage that is both curiously nostalgic and infectiously playful.

In some ways, *RoboCop* does the same. Nonetheless, the Western and science fiction film do share a lot in common: 'not only plot devices and character types but a common setting on the frontier, a common theme of survival, and a common mechanism in which force is sanctioned as a means of survival' (Murray, 1985: 33). Commonality in terms of themes, characters and settings can be overstated but it is Philip French who best explicates why the two genres have characteristically intersected:

> Science fiction and the Western are at once complementary and antithetical forms. Both are concerned with teaching lessons to the present through a rewriting of the past or by explorations of current tendencies projected into the future. (French, 1977: 39)

While *RoboCop* does not rewrite the past, it does project nightmarishly into the future about the present, which is what all great science fiction films do.

Chapter 2: Neo-fascist Corporate Bodies

Self-interest, dehumanisation, the market, free enterprise, profits, privatization, power, greed, the shareholder are just some of the caustic euphemisms often associated with the corporation. In *The Corporation: The Pathological Pursuit of Profit and Power*, Joel Bakan (2004) charts the contemporary economic and political ascent of the corporation in American life as distinctly 'pathological', as somewhat monstrous in its conditioning, unaccountable except to its shareholders, a threat to the public sphere, and arguing that we should 'subject it to democratic constraints and protect citizens from its dangerous tendencies' (Bakan, 2004: 161). It was arguably Reagan and Thatcher, children of Milton Friedman's school of monetary economics, who let the markets reign supreme over both the public and private, creating a toxic state of corporate dread instigating such 'dangerous tendencies'. Beholden to the corporation that impinges on our lives with a terrifying sagacity, it is all but impossible to resist the enslavement we sometimes unconsciously ascribe to corporate power. It seems facetious to label the corporation as the new opium since it can be no longer treated as an addiction as it once was. It is a system, a set of processes, that unconsciously regulates our very existence and for it not to function as it does with such regularity has become a natural phenomenon. But resist we must.

It is the corporation that will form the major focus on this chapter. More specifically, what does the treatment of OCP, the fictional mega-corporation in *RoboCop*, closely linked to fascism, that wields such power and control over the public and private tell us about the way science fiction has represented this ideological development over the years? Furthermore, this chapter will explore the physical effects of the corporation on the individual body, its commodification, dehumanisation and namely Murphy's transformation into a fascistic product. At the same time, just how far does the film go with its critique of the corporation? As it is often suggested, the ending of *RoboCop* manifests an ideological lapse that contradicts the rest of the film's corrosive enquiry of corporate power. *RoboCop* also arrived at a critical juncture in American cinema, at the height of Reaganomics, and is a work that belongs to a cycle of anti-corporate films including *Alien* (1979), *Rollerball* (1978), *Outland, Blade Runner* and *Aliens* that used the science fiction repertoire as a vehicle for contemporaneous anxieties. Accordingly, to what degree can we read *RoboCop* within this context as a popular work of cultural dissent?

The Corporation in the Hollywood Science Fiction Genre

While the corporation lingered menacingly in 1950s Hollywood cinema, it was not until the late 1960s and early 1970s that groups of people and notably individuals were increasingly shown in opposition to the corporation. A realisation of the 1960s counter culture movement was the consolidation of an anti-corporate theme. Unsurprisingly, the 1970s dystopian science fiction film came to host popular corporate anxieties, appropriating the form and practicing allegorical analyses, which framed the corporation as a wholly fascistic, pathological entity. If the science fiction genre emerged as a natural site for corporate critique, films of the New American auteur cinema of the 1970s such as *The Godfather II* (1974) and *The Conversation* (1974) (both directed by Francis Ford Coppola), came to be regarded as metaphorical subterfuge, presenting the corporation as both familial and monstrous. Since many of the new 1970s American auteurs had lived through the failed counter culture movement of the 1960s, a social and political disillusionment, most pertinent in the early 1970s, not only led to a cycle of political paranoia thrillers (*The Parallax View* [1974], *Night Moves* [1975], *Klute, All the Presidents Men* [1976] to name a few) but also intimated the sinful, corrupt corporation in the most populist films of the era including *Star Wars*. By the time *Blade Runner* had been released in 1982, the corporation as the monstrous yet familiar other seemed to have become an altogether palpable convention of the dystopian science fiction film.

But let us take stock of the corporation, returning to Fritz Lang's *Metropolis*,[26] an early expressionist science fiction film, set in a future that was an irrefutable allegorical commentary on a polarised 1920s post-German society. What is instructive about *Metropolis* to later representations of the corporation, especially the cycle of anti-corporate science fiction films in the late 1970s and 1980s, is the extent to which the proletariat worker is situated as a threat to the stability and actuality of the corporation, in this case industrial capitalism. In *Metropolis*, in an attempt to quash the worker's revolt, the industrialist uses a robot, created by diabolical inventor Rotwang, to infiltrate the worker's world. The robot, an extension of corporate hegemony, creates havoc amongst the workers, fulfilling the objective of suppressing dissent.

However, *Metropolis* aims for a decidedly indefinite dénouement, imagining an idealistic union between capital and labour, in which the status quo remains problematically intact. The corporation has continually featured in Hollywood cinema, appearing in several genres, but it seemed almost natural the treatment of such a theme was perfectly suited to the dystopian sub-genre as Hollywood could freely project alternating visions of the corporation, even if they were nightmarishly detached. With the defeat of the counter culture movement at the end of the 1960s, the corporation, reinvigorated, would go onto symbolise the distended conquests of capitalism.

Before I move onto an examination of the corporation in *RoboCop*, it is useful to briefly consider the following mainstream Hollywood science fiction films for their treatment of the corporation; *Alien*, *Outland*, *Blade Runner* and *Aliens*, as I have previously stated, together form a loose cycle of films. In 'Visions of the Future in Science Fiction Films 1970 to 1982', Bruce Franklin argues that none of the fifty films released in the period (1970-82) 'shows a functioning democracy in the future. Many display future societies ruled by some form of conspiracy, monopoly, or totalitarian apparatus' (Franklin, 1990: 22). If the 1970s was plainly an era of embitterment then in filmic terms it was a discordant period of introspection evident in many genres, stretching across the entire spectrum of American cinema including the political thriller, horror, melodrama and science fiction.

It was *Alien* in 1979, a horror-science fiction hybrid, that postulated one of the most radical Hollywood critiques of the corporate capitalist doctrine. *Alien*, the first film in a saga that spans across six films including most recently *Alien Covenant* (2017), depicts warrant officer Ellen Ripley (Sigourney Weaver), the central character of the first four films, in direct conflict with the megacorporation Weyland-Yutani. Mother, the computer that controls the mining vessel the crew inhabit, is a system built by the company. Mother's symbiotic partner, the pathological android Ash (Ian Holm), colludes with the company to try to bring the alien back to Earth safely, at the expense of the human crew if necessary. Judith Newton writes:

> The company in *Alien* represents capitalism in its most systemized, computerized, and dehumanizing form, a fact ironically enforced by the name of the company computer, Mother. (Newton, 1990: 82)

The insidious conspiracy amid the company, the computer and the android describes a mordant corporate paradigm, nastier than the alien creature. Director James Cameron would return to this theme in the sequel *Aliens*, depicting, yet again, the company conspiring against Ripley, this time trying to impregnate her with the Alien creature. In *Alien Woman: The Making of Lt. Ellen Ripley* Gallardo and Smith contend director James Cameron rewrites Ripley as a Reaganite hard body action heroine, 'returning to the terrain of terror, however unwillingly' (2004: 73), a shift which is preceded by the character of Vasquez in the film, 'the epitome of the hypermaculine Reagan era hero' (2004: 96). In this context, the narrative trajectory imitates the earlier Cameron scripted *Rambo: First Blood Part II*. Nonetheless, amongst the Reaganite conservatism of *Aliens* is a subdued anti-corporate premise which would emerge as a key trait in Cameron's science fiction films, signifying 'an attitude of rising mistrust aimed at the monolithic structures considered essential to its capitalist ideology' (Abbott, 1994). Cameron's most recent science fiction *Avatar* (2009) also 'dealt with the power of intergalactic corporations using military might to subordinate indigenous people in order to extract valuable resources' (Kain, 2011). Although it's a theme, which Erik Kain, writing in Forbes, argues has become predictably innate to the genre. If, in *Alien*, Ripley is the only remaining survivor, implying corporate capitalism can only be contested by female intervention, Newton is not convinced by the Utopian gender politics:

> The second fantasy is that white middle class women, once integrated into the world of work will somehow save us from its worst excesses and specifically from its dehumanization. (Newton, 1990: 83)

Susan Sontag, talking about 'the imagination of disaster', argues science fiction carves out a 'utopian fantasy space where all problems are easily solved' (Sontag 1994: 209-25). Questionably, the antipathy amongst the workers and the corporation is 'easily solved' with the eventual destruction of both the android and the company computer, a belated triumph. Yet, the *Alien* films do hypothesise one of the more seditious imaginings of our relationship with the corporation in mainstream American genre cinema.

In 1981, science fiction Western *Outland*, dubbed '*High Noon* in outerspace', reworked *Alien*'s theme of the merciless corporation with a deceptively savage rapt. The final science fiction film I want to briefly mention is Ridley Scott's *Blade Runner*, a work that assembles an equally disparaging portrait of a future America. This time it is the fictional Tyrell Corporation that 'invents replicants in order to have a more pliant labour force' (Ryan & Kellner, 1988: 63) while enunciating 'how capitalism turns humans into machines' (ibid.), two themes that chime accordingly with Murphy's transformation into a product and are likely to have had an influence on RoboCop's representations of the corporate state.

Omni Consumer Products (OCP)

Unlike *Blade Runner* or *Alien* in which the corporation is a fictional projection of anxieties situated in a futuristic dystopian milieu,[27] the corporation in *RoboCop*, Omni Consumer Products (OCP) is set in an undisguised, industrial Detroit landscape that strikes a familiar note with audiences. By not projecting outlandishly into the future and instead depicting a recognisable urban metropolis, the makers of *RoboCop* criticise corporate machinations in a contemporaneous perspective, which in the opinion of scholar Adilifu Nama makes it, along with John Carpenter's *They Live* (1988), one 'of the most radical sf films to emerge in the postindustrial era, explicitly critiquing America's class divisions and the way racial inequality operates to further corporate interests' (Nama, 2008: 113). I want to discuss to what extent this claim can be broadly sustained in relation to the film's contradictory ideologies.

Before I consider the often-discussed opening sequence in which ED-209 malfunctions, the first impressions of corporatism in the film are communicated through the media break news bulletin, which is in turn interrupted by a TV advert for heart transplants. The media break presents Detroit in a larger world of unrest, positing the police union in opposition to OCP. More significantly, OCP is given an authorial voice in the shape of Dick Jones while contrastingly the police union is denied the chance to put across their point of view. The suppression of working class dissent postulates the media as the 'main cultural support' for the 'monopoly capitalism' (Best, 1989: 21) of *RoboCop*. This is a view central to the debate about multinational corporations being allowed to own so much of the mainstream media while using it as an instrument through which to disseminate and propagate a myopic view of the world. The culture industry also finds an unsettling equivocation in the heart transplant advertisement, positing the body as commodity, something that can be replaced or recycled:

> Is it time for that big operation? This may be the most important decision of your life. So come down and talk to one of our qualified surgeons here at the Family Heart Center. We feature the complete Jarvik line. Series Seven Sports Heart by Jensen. Yamaha. You pick the heart. Extended warranties. Financing. Qualifies for health-tax credit. (pause) And remember: we care.

Portraying the heart as a product and its related commodification foreshadows the techno-bodily transformation Murphy will undergo. Not only does this chime with the city of Detroit's corporatisation of public services such as healthcare, but points to the government abandoning the interests of democracy in pursuit of private profiteering. In the advert, there is something terrifying about the debasement of the human body, made altogether more sinister with the background music; it seems almost nightmarish, distressing rather than comforting. And the final line, 'and remember: we care', satirically dents the sincerity invoked by the advert, a contradictory rhetoric of corporate placation.

This broad satirical swipe at American corporatism finds a twisted savagery in the opening boardroom sequence that sees ED-209, an OCP product, slaughter one of the corporate minions in what Dick Jones glibly attributes to as a technological 'glitch'. Writer Ed Neumeier[28] says the idea for this particular sequence came from an MCA corporate meeting in which he fantasised a robot would come in and shoot everyone.

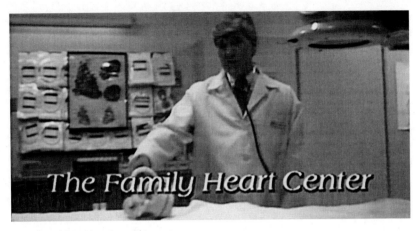

Fig 11. Media Break – Heart Ad

The abrupt cut from the advert back to the media break and straight into the murder of three dead police officers on the streets of Detroit is an ideological juxtaposition in which OCP's negligence as a corporation is contrasted to the caring, empathetic face of corporatism. In some ways, this taps into the schizophrenics of corporate ideology, and the failure of corporatism to live up to its ethical responsibilities in both the public and private sphere in a fair, humane way. If we return to Best's idea, that unruly machinations of capitalism are normalised by the media, the first time we hear the corporation speak in an official context, is filtered through media apparatus in the form of a propitiating sound bite from OCP President Dick Jones:

> Every policeman knows when he joins the force there are certain inherent risks that come with the territory. Ask any cop and he will tell you: 'If you can't stand the heat, you better stay out of the kitchen.'

Jones' corporate diatribe (his words are later made doubly ironic when we discover he is in cahoots with Boddicker) implies police officers are themselves responsible for this crisis since it is a personal commitment that devolves OCP of any accountability. The words are also very glib, dismissing the nobility of the ordinary police officer, reiterating a familiar polarising corporate rhetoric. We can see here the media operating as an extension of corporate hegemony, disseminating the dominant point of view.

After Murphy's formal introduction, the camera follows him as he interacts with his new colleagues, tracking past the showers and finishing in the locker rooms. This sequence vocalises the dissenting anti-OCP sentiments expressed by a number of the police officers: 'They're going to manage this department right into the ground.' Another officer's words emphasises the vulnerability of police officers in receiving adequate medical attention if something should go wrong: 'Yeah, try to get a medevac after you've been jammed.' When one of the more vocal police officers continues with his criticisms of OCP, he argues they should go on strike, only to be interrupted by Reed and the announcement of Frederickson's death.

Nama argues *RoboCop*'s treatment of the police 'symbolizes a Utopian model of blue-collar vitality and class unity that transcends race and gender differences in the face of corporate downsizing' (Nama, 2008: 115). It is corporatism that is demarcated as the enemy, and against which we see an ideological resistance at work, from within the ranks of a working class that shows a united front. Reed sees it differently, arguing as police officers they have a civic duty to the public: 'We're not plumbers. We're police officers. And police officers don't strike.' By positioning Reed in the centre of this conflict between white-collar corporatism and blue-collar working class solidarity Reed takes up the uneasy role of mediator, a vilified position that he will come to question later.

Pronouncements for a strike also underline the corporatisation of public institutions in the 1980s free market liberalism of Reagan's America that saw the erosion of public institutions to effectively carry out their civic obligations; OCP's corporatisation of the Detroit police force lays bare this process. But how should we read Murphy's silence throughout this sequence as he listens to the dissent? Perhaps Murphy is surprised, having been transferred from a much nicer precinct; he suddenly comes face to face with an alternate corporate reality, one that distributes resources to precincts based on locality, affluence and class, reiterating the ways in which corporations protect the interests of their own – the capitalist, ruling elite. The ED-209 sequence formally establishes the official corporate suits of OCP: Dick Jones, Bob Morton, Johnson and the Old Man. I've not included Clarence Boddicker in this paradigm as he exists on the outside in the wilderness, so to speak, but is certainly, as I have stated previously, part of OCP's wider unofficial, corporate universe.

The unveiling of ED-209, 'the future of law enforcement', is preceded by a speech in which Jones situates the development of ED-209 as part of an exploitation of non-profit sectors such as hospitals and prisons. In many ways, the corporatisation of the police appears to be a last bastion. Jones trots out the anticipated corporate spiel, criticising the limitations of the human factor, arguing for the 24-hour police officer, a machine. But ED-209 is more than a machine; he is a 'military product' who has been programmed for the role of 'urban pacification', a grotesque term implying repressive state apparatus and harking back to the Vietnam War. Jones has developed ED-209 solely as a corporate product with plans for wider national and global distribution yet fails to account for the way new technology often backfires. In this case, the death of Mr. Kinney, a corporate newbie, at the hands of ED-209, referred to Jones as a 'glitch', is a moment of violence Verhoeven orchestrates with a satirical symbolic quip – Kinney's eviscerated body falling back onto the model of Delta City.

Even more troubling, in this moment of tragedy, Bob Morton takes advantage of the situation, managing to argue a claim for his RoboCop programme to the Old Man. This cutthroat world of white corporate men is one that the film seeks to ridicule especially in the projections of fascistic technology. All of the corporate suits are depicted as unscrupulous 'scumbags' (a term first used by Reed moments before) in their contempt for human life. Yet the framing of Jones, Morton and the Old Man, in OCP HQ and the boardroom, is unavoidably linked to the rather iconic use of glass, an architectural symbol often associated with the corporate world and stereotypical of Hollywood corporate imaginings. Glass in this context evokes transparency, a patina of clarity masking the corrupt corporatism of OCP while alternately attributing an omniscient gaze to the corporate world, the all-seeing Jones and Morton of OCP, masters of their cosmos.

Body Politics

The creation of RoboCop stems out of OCP's quick fix attempts to resolve crime in Detroit. Jones, the pathological face of corporatism, sees ED-209 as a military product. Unlike ED-209, which is a purely technological construct, RoboCop's fusion of man and machine emerges as a terrifying allegory for corporate enslavement. It is Murphy's conversion into a product that functions most readily as a satirical commentary on the insidious ways in which corporations subjugate us into thinking they are working in our best interests. RoboCop is created along such totalitarian lines. Thereby, Murphy's transformation into RoboCop is a site of body politic contestation in the film's narrative, and it is a body subject to corporate processes: technification, commodification, and finally fetishisation. I want to explore a few of these ideas further, focusing initially on the birth of RoboCop.

When the doctors in the operating room call time on Murphy, a cut to black signifies his death. The soundtrack also falls silent, confirming the termination of Murphy. The sequence retains the cut to black until it is interrupted by a series of glitches that we often see when tuning in a TV set or a radio. This fuzzy subjective point of view shot presents a marked shift in our position as spectator, which has in large part up to now remained within an auxiliary position, looking in on the world being constructed for us. This shift to a fixed vantage point occurs at a critical moment, letting us directly witness the birth of RoboCop. Moreover, the effect on the spectator is eerie to say the least, creating a doubling in which we are also subjected to the experience of looking on powerlessly as the corporation claims our bodies. This moment sutures us into the narrative action on a sensory plane, whereby we forge an adopted connection with Murphy. From now on we see the world through his eyes, enslaved by OCP.

When Morton chastises his team for saving Murphy's arm, he turns to Johnson for corporate sanction who says, 'He signed release forms when he joined the force. He's legally dead. We can do pretty much what we want to.' Johnson's officious reasoning reconnects the film back to the loose paradigm of anti-corporate science fiction cinema since it reframes the blue collar protagonist as an expendable by product of the corporate universe. Trapped behind the prism of a computer interface we can only but listen to the corporation dictate terms and claim Murphy's body with impunity. 'That the state of the body is the state of the nation is a notion set deep in the American psyche' (Larson, 2004: 197), one that resonates if we read RoboCop's quest to reclaim his identity as connected to the corpus of body politics.

In terms of film theory, the body politic is often situated in Susan Jefford's 'hard body' examination of the relationship between Hollywood masculinity and 1980s American action films. While RoboCop's 'hard body' projects a Reaganite fascist aesthetic, I want to propose RoboCop's quest to reclaim his body/identity can in fact be viewed as a feminist act. To do so requires the term body politic be traced back to the second wave of the 1970s feminist movement where it was first used to emphasise a woman's control over her body. It may seem contradictory to claim an overly masculine text such as *RoboCop* could accommodate a potential feminist reading. But this demands we read the massacre of Murphy as a form of bodily rape, expressed viscerally via the disturbing image of an eviscerated body. If a societal constituent, an unlawful mob, perpetrates this rape then OCP's claiming of Murphy's body and subsequent mutilation could be construed as corporate rape. RoboCop's quest to reclaim his body/identity is in fact first initiated by the intervention of Lewis, the only significant female character in the film. Ideologically, this female intervention is vital to a feminist reading of RoboCop's reclamation of his body. The major difficulty with this feminist reading is that Lewis is not given opportunity to develop, reduced to fulfilling a narrative function, raising questions about the film's hegemonic gender roles.

Corporate Threshold

'What are they gonna do? Replace us?' is one of the reactions from the police officers upon seeing RoboCop for the first time, while another emphasises the technological ramifications: 'He's not a guy, he's a machine.' RoboCop's introduction into the police precinct, an operational base for OCP, coincides with the looming prospect of strike action by the Detroit police. The fear of the blue-collar worker replaced by a technological machine that can do a job more proficiently was a prevalent source of unease in the 1980s. Nama writes:

> The forward march of capitalism would include a technological overhaul that, in many cases, would make factory labourers redundant in assembly-line manufacturing plants, regardless of their race. (Nama, 2010: 117)

Since corporate men like Bob Morton only care for the bottom line, the creation of RoboCop is about eradicating the worker's political consciousness; the will to resist and question authority. This is what takes place when OCP blank Murphy's memory, expunging doubt, anxiety and dissent, temporarily producing a police officer as a somnambulistic neo-fascist corporate slave:

> For the master to be killed, for the master-slave relationship to end, the slave too must cease to be a slave. He must somehow discover his lost humanity and fashion it in his image. (Bulhan, 1985: 104)

However, the human consciousness is a complex system, one that OCP arrogantly assumes they have mastered through multifarious corporate machinations. The creation of both ED-209 and RoboCop also arises from the larger corporate goal, Delta City, which is behind schedule because Old Detroit is ridden with crime, a natural by-product of an unequal culture. The hope to implement the RoboCop program stems from capitalist expansionism, a key ideological signifier in the paradigm of dystopian science fiction cinema. As I pointed out earlier, the moment at which corporation machinations are first questioned and begin to break down is the sequence in which RoboCop recalls fragments of a past memory that leads to a re-awakening. Let us take a closer look at this sequence.

It opens with a shot of an ECG machine, specially constructed to monitor the vitals of RoboCop, tracking his bio data. This shot reminds us of the totalising regulation of RoboCop's man-machine body by the corporation. And while OCP may be in control of his body they cannot account for the metaphysical, something that can never be regulated. The next shot, a master shot, makes striking use of deep focus. The background is taken up by the cage in which RoboCop is imprisoned; he is asleep, his head pointing to the floor. In the middle ground of the frame we see two scientists in white coats. Both are reading newspapers. In this same middle ground of the frame we also see RoboCop's offline image reproduced on two TV monitors. This simulacra effect of RoboCop reproduced in three images foreshadows what is about to take place: the fracturing of identity. The foreground part of the frame is taken up by the ECG machine, which is now mapped geographically in the space. A young woman and corporate suit enters the frame marking the ECG while declining one of the

Fig 12. RoboCop goes online

scientist's offer for food. We next cut to a shot of RoboCop, framed in a high angle medium close-up. Although he is offline, his left hand and fingers begins to twitch indicating disturbance. He is clearly dreaming. The next shot cuts back to the initial shot that was used to open the sequence; this time the ECG begins recording the disturbances on the paper. In a standard moment of continuity editing, the next shot cuts back to RoboCop in the cage, but this time opting for an acute high angle. The choice of the high angle and the opening up of the shot to a mid-shot ostensibly extenuates RoboCop's overbearing mechanical status. He twitches again, this time more violently. Cutting back to the scientists who are still distracted by their newspapers, the demarcation of physical space between RoboCop, the neo-fascist technological slave, and OCP, is inscribed by the cage, a public-corporate threshold. This medium wide-angle shot repeats the disruptive effect of reproducing RoboCop's image. In the two empty monitors below we see the distorted image of Clarence Boddicker appear, a memory recalled from RoboCop's past, the deceased Murphy. The image of Boddicker is the one Murphy last saw before his death: of Boddicker pointing a gun at him. As we cut back to RoboCop's reaction, a close-up is used to magnify his torment of remembering a past that has resurfaced. The spectral image of Boddicker is clarified with the next shot, a flashback insert of Boddicker holding his shotgun and readying to shoot and dismember Murphy's hand. We cut back to RoboCop in a close-up again, his agonising torment and re-awakening coming to fruition. The next shot cuts back to Boddicker firing the shotgun; the trauma of this memory is registered dissonantly on the soundtrack and explicated by cutting to RoboCop's tormented reaction. The rupturing of this past trauma also brings back the memories of his other assailants, Boddicker's goons, who are inserted into the sequence, the editing pattern intercutting from the past and present in an increasingly aggressive manner.

As the scientists finally realise what is going on, a series of sharp edits are used to depict RoboCop finally rising from his chair. This moment culminates with a flashback insert of Boddicker, his gun aimed at us, and the point at which Boddicker killed Murphy. When the scientists glibly say 'Hey look, Bucket boy's online', RoboCop's awakening is brought to an end with the insert of Boddicker's gunfire once again experienced by RoboCop's discombobulated state. After the ECG reading goes back to normal, we cut to another high angle shot, the sharpest of the sequence, framing

RoboCop as a leviathan. In the next shot, the petrified scientists look on helplessly as RoboCop opens the cage. Emphasising the significance of this action, RoboCop's hand is framed in a close-up as he pulls across the door to the cage and then exits.

It is here in this micro action of the pulling across of the cage door we see the violation of the public-corporate threshold. RoboCop's revolt and liberation from the cage indicates a transgression, a first attempt to defy corporate constraints by crossing over into the public space through an act of will power. Read ideologically, it is complicated to fully view this act as the corporate slave taking the first step towards liberation especially given the dubious politics of the ending. But RoboCop's departure from the cage throws the technology of OCP used to monitor and control into disarray, posing the orthodox question about technophobia often duplicated by dystopian science fiction cinema. Later, the scientists have no logical way of accounting for what they have just witnessed. But Morton angrily rubbishes the suggestion that RoboCop had a dream since it permits for a metaphysical reasoning that goes outside the uncontrollable sphere of the corporation.

The final part of this sequence sees RoboCop interact with Lewis for the first time since his death. As he exits the cage, making his way through the back of the precinct, we first see Lewis through RoboCop's technologised point of view, lines running across the impersonal image. Lewis turns and goes after RoboCop, stepping into his field of vision, asking, 'Do you have a name?' In what has to be one of the most cryptic shots in the film, RoboCop's taciturn reaction to Lewis's question is explicated in a tight symmetrical close up that construes uncertainty, chiming logically with the identity crisis he is now facing. The rest of this encounter between Lewis and RoboCop is played out through a series of alternating point of view shots, creating an unusual level of subjectivity that sees us identifying with both of the characters. Communication through the shared space of the point of view shot in this encounter implies Lewis and RoboCop are connected by a blue-collar solidarity that undercuts the sense of corporate control enacted over technology. When Lewis explicitly states, 'Murphy, it's you', speaking to his repressed incorporeal consciousness, RoboCop's reaction of stepping back as if to take stock of this encumbered statement is a non verbal recognition that contemplatively puts him in opposition to the motives of OCP.

Fig 13. Murphy, it's you

In turn, Lewis's questioning of RoboCop leads to Morton criticising the police department for their interference in corporate matters, rebuking Lewis – 'Let me make it clear for you. He doesn't have a name. He's got a program. He's product' – thereby undermining any attempts to claim RoboCop as a blue-collar worker. The ideological contest amid OCP and the Detroit police in claiming ownership of RoboCop is also representative of a struggle to define and hold on to a working class identity threatened by extinction from corporatisation. Morton's accusatory tone, which is completely unsympathetic to the problems of the police officers, is augmented by his deprecating choice of language, referring to them as 'grunts'. And to reassert the rule of OCP as a corporation that functions and acts detachedly Morton states with equivocation to Reed, 'This project doesn't concern cops. It's classified. It's OCP.' In a way, RoboCop's unplanned departure from the cage necessitates the corporation's want to re-draw the public-private threshold that has just been threatened. This functions broadly as an ideological reaction from the corporation, to reinforce the status quo and quash working class dissent as symbolised by Lewis's transgression.

Corporate Machinations

The final aspect of this chapter entails a closer study of the corporate rivalry between Jones and Morton, which forms a major source of dramatic interest, advancing the narrative. There are four sequences that are of significance to us Jones and Morton's homoerotic encounter in the executive lounge, Boddicker's slaying of Morton at the behest of Jones, RoboCop's attempt to apprehend Jones for aiding Boddicker, and lastly, the final shootout in the OCP boardroom. Although I have already analysed the ending in relation to a genre reading in terms of the Western, I want to return to the final moments of the film since they can be read in complicatedly alternate ways when viewed through a corporate prism.

The successful launch of the RoboCop program, supported by a pliant media, results in Bob Morton promoted to Vice President of Security Concepts. Since Morton trumps Jones with his RoboCop program, the intense rivalry between the two of them is encapsulated in a confrontation in the executive washroom. This sequence begins with Morton being congratulated by one of his colleagues, another executive. Before entering the washroom, in a moment of yuppie self-aggrandisement Morton and his fellow executive smugly clink their gold cards, celebrating Morton's acceptance in to a painfully white corporate club. The capacity to gain access to another part of the corporate world is characteristic of most corporate hierarchies in which the allocation of divisions creates a tiered system that engenders a desire for mobility in terms of accumulating power. All of this is visualised in Morton's supercilious Yuppie persona. Upon entering the washroom, the camera pans from right to left tracking Morton and his colleague as they walk over to the urinals. The camera position in the panning shot is placed literally on the floor of the toilets. As the camera finishes its pan of the washroom it comes to a stop at the feet of Dick Jones who is in one of the cubicles, suitably taking a dump. The staging of this confrontation in a washroom may seem a little unusual but the most subversive ideological comparison is the one that blurs the line between human and capitalist waste, they co-exist in this nightmarish corporate paradigm. Furthermore, the inclusion of stock market tickers conveniently placed over the urinals realises a satirical comment on the corporate space as interminable.

Morton begins to bemoan the unimportance of Jones, referring to him as a 'pussy', and mocking him further with a quip about his old age. A group of executives realise Jones is in the cubicle and exit promptly. When Jones exits the cubicle, the cowardly executive who has just been laughing with Morton at Jones also exits hastily, not before we see he has amusingly 'pissed his pants' in dread. The enmity between Jones and Morton is primarily a pathological condition imitated by the corporate world. But the recrimination from Jones is also predicated on gender anxieties. In what is an aggressively masculine space, Morton calls Jones a 'pussy', a mark of emasculation. The only way Jones can contain the unbridled ego of Morton is to eliminate him. Note when Boddicker slays Morton he has Boddicker shoot him in the legs. In the film noir universe, masculine impairment is often linked to impotency, and in this context, this symbolic action of shooting Morton in the legs is an ideological neutering of Morton's new unchecked masculinity. This killing of Morton permits Jones to reassert his threatened masculinity, refracting the gender politics of the 1980s male dominated corporate universe, certainly a rejoinder to the 1970s feminist movement. The sequence ends with a homoerotic frisson. Jones begins by running his hand across Morton's hair only to violently pull it back, reasserting his dominance over the corporate space and warning Morton of the implications of his hostile deportment.

RoboCop's attempt to arrest Dick Jones at OCP HQ elucidates further corporate machinations. Jones anticipates the arrival of RoboCop via a mobile tracking device, another technological symbol of corporate omniscience. Upon entering the building, RoboCop plays back the video recording of Boddicker incriminating Jones. 'Don't you get it. I work for Dick Jones. He runs OCP. OCP runs the cops,' pleads a shredded

Boddicker. When RoboCop attempts to arrest Jones, he is prevented from doing so by a 'product violation', which results in the paralysis of RoboCop. Reducing RoboCop to the corporate puppet that he is, reminds us that any attempts to enact the law with equivocation does not apply to the corporate sphere, that corporate ideologues like Jones circumvent the system so to remain above the law. Jones refers to directive four as an 'insurance policy', that 'any attempt to arrest a senior office of OCP results in shutdown'. Unlike human police officers that can still question, dissent and go on strike, directive four is programmed to eliminate accountability of the corporation but more importantly keep in check the status quo. It is a pre-programmed method of political acquiescence.

Prior to this confrontation with Jones, RoboCop's technological indestructibility has been repeatedly emphasised, unequivocally in the warehouse shootout. The dominant aura of RoboCop, the invincible robot, is projected with such potency that when he finally comes undone by Jones' Machiavellian shenanigans, RoboCop is powerless to do anything. This becomes the first occasion when we witness RoboCop's fallibility returning him to the civilian world. This is also a turning point in the film's narrative, marking RoboCop's journey to reject his cyborg identity, which is made altogether powerful when at first ED-209 tries to kill him (the clash of robots is a measure of the science fiction cyborg film and one that I will return to) and later his own fellow police officers; both at the behest of Jones. Parallels are drawn yet again between the pathological villainy of Jones and Boddicker who are determined to hold onto power at whatever costs, distorting the line between the corporate and criminal world. What RoboCop's clash with Jones also returns to is his vulnerability as a police officer. Though he is resurrected as a commoditised technological entity, and stripped of his mystique, RoboCop is in fact just as expendable as his human counterparts. Reading this sequence as an obliteration of RoboCop's heroic status reaches back to Murphy's imaginings of the cowboy, which was challenged by Boddicker. Demythologising heroic assumptions is linked by the unsavoury Jones-Boddicker alliance, and intrinsic to RoboCop/Murphy's quest to reclaim an identity that has been expunged by the corporation.

Corporate Acquiescence

In this last part of the chapter I want to return to the ending previously analysed in terms of genre. The ending to *RoboCop* can be read in ideologically alternate ways. In terms of corporate power, while RoboCop confronts Jones, exacting revenge, OCP as a system remains very much intact. Booker writes:

> Murphy, in the final analysis, remains Murphy despite the high-tech hardware that has replaced his physical body. In this sense, *RoboCop* is a relatively conventional, conservative, and uninventive film. (Booker, 2006: 211)

Although I disagree with Booker's comments about the film's conventional and uninventive nature, the conservatism Booker identifies is evident in RoboCop's refusal to completely overthrow the corporation. Ideologically, the ending is where the film is most ambivalent about the politics of the day, and in some respects dubiously preserves the status quo; the Old Man remains at the helm.

In the build up to the ending, Lewis helps RoboCop to defeat Boddicker and his goons in a violent gun battle at the steel mill, which results in RoboCop killing Boddicker. And as Lewis lies wounded, she cries out, 'Murphy, I'm a mess'. RoboCop's defeatist rejoinder, 'They'll fix you, they fix everything', becomes a final metonym for the ubiquitous corporate system and the processes it deploys to placate and subdue the masses. RoboCop's noted emphasis on OCP being able to 'fix everything' is also significant since it raises the question about corporate corruption, of which Jones is a prime example, while confirming the sense of betrayal Murphy feels by the corporation as he was targeted and transformed into a machine. Also, the wider ideological implication is that the corporation regulates every facet of our lives, determining identity, choice, lifestyle and even morality.

Next, as RoboCop drives to OCP HQ, Jones addresses the board of executives, arguing they take advantage of the strike, undermining proletariat unionism. 'By the end of the week we can have ED-209s in place in the city and expect immediate public support,' exalts Jones. With Morton out of the way, Jones has the impunity to push through his original ED-209 military project. While Morton was a vicious corporate lackey, compared to Jones, Morton strikes us as the lesser of two evils in this corporate quagmire. Naturally, the opportunism of Jones, exploiting the proletariat cause, and seeking to undermine the strike is demonstrative of a larger corporate agenda that actively sought to dismantle organised labour in the 1980s; a result of what Noam Chomsky calls the 1960s excess of democracy. 'I've got one downstairs, guarding the building now,' says Jones, trying to restore the board's faith in his dreaded project. RoboCop pulls up outside OCP HQ in his battered police car and is confronted by ED-209: 'You are illegally parked on private property. You have 20 seconds to move your vehicle.' Before ED-209 can take action, RoboCop blows the lumbering behemoth into smithereens, leaving only his legs; a mutilated ED-209 spins and falls down flat in a cartoonish affectation.

RoboCop's annihilation of ED-209 suggests many political interpretations. Firstly, since ED-209 is a technological projection of Jones's masculinity and power, this demolition acts as a precursor to the unmasking of Jones in the boardroom, stripping Jones of a political immunity. Secondly, ED-209 poses a threat to the police force in terms of jobs so RoboCop's symbolic annihilation of this potential threat can be viewed in political terms as a form of resistance, enacting solidarity with striking police colleagues. Lastly, the destruction of ED-209 undermines Jones' prior corporate sentiments about technology as protection while ridiculing suggestions of technology as a solution to the social problems of crime. Having destroyed ED-209, the sequence continues, this time cutting back to Jones still pontificating in the boardroom: 'because this corporation will live up to the guiding principles of its founder. Courage. Strength. Conviction. We will meet each new challenge with the same aggressive attitude.' And just as Jones delivers these final words, there is a brazen edit to RoboCop swinging open the doors to the boardroom in a grand dramatic gesture, a transgression of the public-corporate threshold, yielding a potent irony.

RoboCop's declaration that 'Dick Jones is wanted for murder' disrupts the corporate inviolability of the boardroom. Inserting his bloodied mechanical spike into the computer portal, playing back video evidence that explicates proof of Jones' guilt. Technology turning against its corporate masters is made doubly oracular in this denouement. Jones reacts with desperation, taking the Old Man hostage, demanding a helicopter. Only by firing Jones can RoboCop take action, which he does, shooting Jones several times, before his dead body falls back out of a glass window. The conventional iconography of the shattered window articulates Jones is ejected from the corporate world in the most violent of ways. Yet while one would assume the corporate world of OCP has been shaken irrefutably, the Old Man is indebted to RoboCop's intervention, acknowledging his public service and duty as a police officer. This acknowledgment is posited ambiguously; has RoboCop acted in the interests of the public or the corporation? By shooting dead Jones RoboCop ensures OCP is temporarily protected from corrupt machinations, which, of course, works in the favour of the corporate world. But while the Old Man assumes RoboCop is still an OCP product, the declaration of the name 'Murphy' rejects any attempts to claim RoboCop as part of the corporate world. Is it now that RoboCop belongs to neither worlds nor ideologies, that his liberation no longer posits him as a neo-fascist corporate slave?

Figure 14. Nice shooting, son

If we take a comparative approach, likening the ending of *RoboCop* to *Rambo First Blood: II*, another hard body action film of the same era, some useful political adoptions become evident. At the end of *Rambo*, upon returning to the base Rambo takes his gun and shoots up the technological machinery that has been governing the mission. Russell Berman points out that Rambo's real enemy is the 'governmental machine, with its massive technology, unlimited regulations, and venal political motivations. Rambo is the anti-bureaucratic non-conformist opposed to the state, the new individual activist' (Berman, 1985: 145). Rambo's decimation of this machinery is a spectacular symbolic overture and conceals a rage against the system that he recognises cannot be validated by killing Murdoch, the man in charge of operations. Rambo's opposition to the state is kept in check, mainly through the mediating presence of Colonel Trautman (Richard Crenna), finding parallels in RoboCop's augmented restraint in the boardroom at the end.

Unlike Rambo, who is a drifter, an outsider and is able to walk away from situations, RoboCop is still part of an inescapable corporate world. Nonetheless, RoboCop's very presence in the corporate boardroom transgresses the public-corporate threshold, which in itself could be deemed as representative of blue-collar dissatisfaction with Reagan's economically polarised America. The fantasy wish fulfilment reading of the ending to *RoboCop* finds notable parallels with *Rambo*, a film that re-imagined the trauma of the Vietnam War by controversially positing America as the victors. *RoboCop* operates along similar ideological lines, offering audiences a gratifying form of expiation and catharsis, an audience pleasure often derived from popular film genres:

> RoboCop's ability to walk into a corporate boardroom and blow away the company's most evil executive surely resonated with a number of working-class fantasies of the 1980s, allowing workers of America's declining industries to imagine revenge against the heartless corporations that were gradually depriving them of their jobs and their lives. (Booker, 2006: 212)

In this wider context of working class fantasy RoboCop's confrontation and slaying of Jones is radical indeed, validating the film's vehement critique of corporate capitalist ideology. Thus, RoboCop's final reassertion of his real human identity, Murphy, the blue-collar police officer, is one that also resonates, since this position defies OCP's attempts to treat RoboCop as a product.

Satirising the Mainstream Media

Some fans of *RoboCop* recognise that the satirical aspects are equally significant as the genre elements, and in some respects the darkly satirical tone is an abiding refrain of Verhoeven's American science fiction work. The satirical edge of *RoboCop* is what makes the film particularly distinctive in the Hollywood science fiction canon, and compared to its cyborg brethren, which all have an unmistakable stoicism to their unsmiling narratives, *RoboCop* functions more like a satirical text, deconstructing the absurdities of Reagan's America. The final section of this chapter will examine the satirical aspects of *RoboCop*, considering the relationship to 1980s Reaganite America, mainstream media culture, and the consolidation of neoliberalism as the next phase of capitalist advancement and societal ruin.

It is worth mentioning the satirical edge in *RoboCop* is defined early on with the comical tone struck by the media break inserts. While much of the satire is focused on sending up the banality of American popular culture, an abiding refrain is Bixby Snyder's catchphrase 'I'd buy that for a dollar'. This memorable catchphrase comes from a trashy fictional TV show that everyone seems to be watching in the film. Bixby Snyder riotously delivers the catchphrase in a gaudy close up through a personalised direct camera address. The catchphrase seems to epitomise a ruined, superfluous dystopian culture in which capitalism is ridiculed but also determines the lifeblood of its lowly inhabitants. On two occasions in the film, we find Emil watching the show, delighted by the humour, and accordingly Emil's familiar reaction humanises his menacing character. The satire that underlines the corporate address in the film is not restricted solely to OCP, but also emerges from Boddicker and his goons, notably Emil. An early exchange between Emil and Dougy, a fellow criminal who gets wasted by Murphy, relates and legitimises the principle of free enterprise, a defining characteristic of Reaganomics, as no different to theft:

Dougy: 'We keep robbin' banks but we never get to keep the money.'
Emil: 'Takes money to make money. We steal money to buy coke then sell the coke to make even more money. Capital investment, man.'
Dougy: 'Yeah, but why bother making it when we can just steal it?'
Emil: 'No better way to steal money than free enterprise.'

Emil's probing words are unconventionally astute for a lowlife criminal. Yet such economic acumen tells us the line between the corporate and criminal world is horribly vague, implying the Jones-Boddicker equation is altogether habitual in Reagan's unscrupulous economics model. It is worth noting Emil's character is one of the most memorable in *RoboCop* mainly because Paul McCrane's performance is despicably funny. Much of this dark humour extends from Emil's unruliness; he simply takes whatever he wants: 'Give me all your money, bookworm, or I'll blow your brains out,' says Emil to the attendant working at the petrol station that he robs. The nerdy gas attendant who is learning geometry comments sarcastically on the pointlessness of education in a world ruled by violence. Emil reminds the attendant of Reagan's new American economic politics in which social mobility is a non-existent farce: 'I bet you think you're pretty smart, huh? Think you could outsmart a bullet?' In the late 1980s America was beginning to emerge as a militarised society, although guns and violence were intrinsically a defining feature in the history of America. Emil's marauding presence is a satirical dissection of Reagan's unchecked economic system; he is the free market which no one can contain or bring to account. The only way to stop Emil is to kill him.

Media Break[29]

There are three media breaks, short news bulletins made up of hard and soft news content, which are in turn interrupted by advertisements. The media break acts as a structuring device, breaking up the logical flow of the narrative, while acting as a conduit for corporate America and a commentary on 1980s geopolitics and a sensationalist news culture satirised in the film: 'You give us three minutes and we'll give you the world', says Casey Wong and Jess Perkins, the jovial anchors. The first media break, used at the opening of the film, begins with a story about Pretoria, referencing what was then the racial politics of apartheid South Africa:

> The threat of nuclear confrontation in South Africa escalated today when a ruling white military government of that besieged city state unveiled a French made neutron bomb and affirmed its willingness to use the three megaton device as the city's last line of defence.

In the early 1980s Mikhail Gorbachev had announced *perestroika*[30] and nuclear disarmament seemed increasingly likely in the coming years. But even though the cold war was thawing, the threat of nuclear confrontation was still disseminated by much of the mainstream US media. The Pretoria news story imagines a nightmarish racial civil war in which there is an implied alliance amongst ruling white governments countering the threat of a black uprising through direct military force and intervention.

The seriousness of this news story is undercut by the subsequent soft news story in which the President's press conference in outer space leads to a period of weightlessness. 'The Star Wars orbiting peace platform' which the story refers to was Reagan's Strategic Defense Initiative, launched in 1984, a space-based anti-missile system, famously mocked by the media as 'Star Wars'. The light-heartedness of this soft news story is often found at the end of news programmes, placating the audience with a happy ending, which has often led to accusations that the mainstream media cultivates political inertia. Reagan's persona was a filmic construction, and many of his speeches and initiatives were deliberately staged to invoke the visual iconography of popular American cinema. Never before had an American president depended so brazenly on the ubiquity of the image as a false mythology.

The media break then cuts to an ad break for a prosthetic replacement heart, discussed earlier in Chapter 1, and concludes with the news story of Officer Frank Frederickson's fight to stay alive. This is followed with Dick Jones telling us about the inherent risks faced by police officers in Detroit and the identification of Clarence Boddicker as the main suspect in Frederickson's shooting. As a show of support for Frank Frederickson, Casey Wong ends the news broadcast with a patronising 'Good luck, Frank!'. As discussed in Chapter 3, the media do not give the police officers a voice in the news story, which is in contrast to OCP's presence through Dick Jones who is permitted to defend the corporate position. The media breaks are a primary tool of political coercion, reinstating the status quo and manufacturing consent, manipulating the sentiments of the viewers.

The film continually satirises ideological coercion, and in the second media break, the news media as an instrument for corporate propaganda is apparent in the valorisation of OCP's 'revolutionary crime-management programme'. This first news story sees RoboCop visiting Lee Iacocca Elementary School, an obvious PR exercise, in which the kids are shown interacting with RoboCop. When asked by a reporter for any special message for the kids watching at home, RoboCop says 'Stay out of trouble'. The media's representation of RoboCop as some kind of saviour figure, humanising his strangeness through the connection with children, certainly satirises the notions of hero worship and comic book fantasies deployed by the mainstream media to satiate the mass public. A prevailing theme of Reagan's 1980s America was the militarisation of the police force, much of it problematically justified by Congress in light of the supposedly endemic War on Drugs. RoboCop 'has crooks on the run in Old Detroit', as stated in the news report, reiterating the contributory role of the mainstream media, legitimising inexact aspects of domestic policy in the public realm.

The next story is a hard news affair: 'American troops participated in a joint raid with Mexican nationals against rebel rocket positions in Acapulco.' In 1986 Ronald Reagan passed the Immigrant Reform and Control Act (IRCA), re-politicising the crisis of Mexican cross-border immigration as a threat to the national security of America. In what appears to be the destabilisation of Mexico, the US is presented as aiding the Mexican government in trying to suppress what is a rebellion. Once again, this is contradictory to Reagan's murderous and imperialist interventionist foreign policies in Latin America. But the disparity between the stark political reality of Reagan's 1980s America and the propagandistic nature of the mainstream news media points to a significant disconnect in which the media is complicit in the sanitisation of the American government as pragmatic and cautious when it comes to foreign intervention. In this context, the complicated ideological constructions of the media breaks demythologise the dubious machinations of a monolithic, servile news culture. Before the final news item in the media break, we cut to another advertisement, this time a perverse twist on the familiar board game. The ad titled 'NUKEM', with the tagline 'Get them before they get you!' features a family exchanging bullish geopolitical comments in their living room, satirising a warped culture of war, militarisation and most potently, nuclear confrontation:

> You crossed my line of death!
> You haven't dismantled your MX stockpile!
> Pakistan is threatening my border!
> That's it, buster, no more military aid!

After this exchange, a metonym of the way nuclear mobilisation in the late 1980s had created an anxious international climate of discord, the ad culminates in a small explosion generated by the game itself and a mushroom cloud. In what is one of the more remarkably outlandishly brilliant moments in the film, NUKEM communicates, with the darkest of comical overtones, the culture industry and its role in normalising and naturalising violence, death and nuclear war for the ordinary American family, prophesying that it may inevitably become an accepted part of everyday reality for Americans.

The third and final media break begins with an ad promoting a car. The ad finds a dinosaur rampaging through the streets as people flee in panic. But when the dinosaur comes across something much bigger than itself, a car of all things (the 6000 SUX), the dinosaur cannot believe what it sees, and recoils in astonishment. The ad is juxtaposed with the following VO commentary: 'It's back. Big is back. Because bigger is better. 6000 SUX. An American tradition.' The ad ends with the image of the 6000 SUX looming over both the city and the dinosaur. Like the NUKEM advert before it, the 6000 SUX ad can be read as ridiculing an absurdist American culture industry geared to selling consumerist goods in the most banal fashions. The polluting, hyperbolic image of the 6000 SUX is a social aberration, fetishised as a consumerist totem in the film, epitomising the rock bottom state of play in Reagan's America. Later we see Clarence eviscerate a 6000 SUX into a fireball, another metaphor for the self-destructiveness of neoliberal capitalism.

The next news story mourns the death of 113 people including two former presidents in the Santa Barbara area, the result of a laser cannon misfiring on board the Strategic Defense Peace Platform. The continuing reference to Reagan's Star Wars project is even more explicit in this news story and warns of the potential dangers of a defence system reliant on modern technology. Once again, the darkly satirical tone, ridiculing the exaggerated paranoia and anxiety induced by the outrageous politics of the cold war, suggests the counter-productive nature of such systems actually puts at risk the well being and safety of ordinary Americans. While the technological glitch projects a nightmarish futuristic scenario, the fallibility of technology and the human cost at stake recalls the opening mishaps of Dick Jones and ED-209 in the OCP boardroom.

The third media break concludes with a story on the looming police strike action including a reporter interviewing people 'in the crime plagued Lexington area'. The first interviewee, Peter Whitley, a homeowner says: 'They're public servants. They got job security. They're not supposed to strike,' conveying a civic disenchantment, manipulatively amplified by the media. The second interviewee, Keva Rosenberg, an unemployed person, says:

It's a free society. Except there ain't nothing free because there's no guarantees. You're on your own. It's the law of the jungle.

Like earlier, the views of the police officers are never shown, staging an image of the strike as one of disobedience and negligence, suggesting chaos will reign. The news report distorts a wider corporate liability in the looming strike, displacing the crisis as one solely instigated by the police force. And the choice of words by the first interviewee creates resentment about the strike, which the mainstream news media emphasises in order to delegitimise the police officers right to strike. The perpetual cultural currency of Rosenberg's words is the most instructive, pointing to the lawlessness inherent within a so-called free neoliberal society, which privileges individual contestation and survival over collectivism. When the police force is so close to the private sphere, controlled by the corporations, civil liberties lose their value.

The media breaks unmask the ideological state apparatus at the disposal of the ruling elite. And by satirising the apparatus, showing in this instance how the news media operates to disseminate dominant ideologies, it becomes patent that winning the consent of the masses is a continual political practice. In some ways, even RoboCop/ Murphy is oblivious to the subtle practices of ideological coercion, implying his failure to directly confront OCP points to the triumph of corporate power. Nonetheless, most dystopian science fiction films foreground the spectacle, but *RoboCop* does the opposite, which makes the film a uniquely cultural artefact, uncovering a political system that most Hollywood films rarely want to engage with.

The Coke Factory

Film culture often remembers *RoboCop* for the shoot 'em up sequence in the coke factory. Producer Jon Davison says the coke factory was their homage to the Italian Western. While it is an action-oriented sequence with lots of swanky exploding squibs and A-Team style goons populating the grubby *mise-en-scène*, the satirical intent of situating a confrontation between RoboCop and the criminal elements of Old Detroit in a cocaine factory is significant to the historical context of the mid- to late 1980s when urban American communities saw an explosion of crack cocaine.

It was Richard Nixon who in the 1970s made drug abuse a national issue, mainly for electoral reasons. With the introduction of crack cocaine in the mid-1980s, fuelling an epidemic of users and sellers, the War on Drugs was accelerated by Ronald Reagan's hard line stance, pushing through the Anti-Drug Abuse Act, which enacted punitive mandatory minimum sentences for drug-related crimes. In Reagan's era, the disproportionate levels of black people incarcerated for the possession of drugs, particularly crack cocaine increased exponentially. In the bind of national hysteria created by the advent of crack cocaine was the complicit role of law enforcement, congress and the mainstream media, which colluded to amplify the threat posed by drugs to civil society. A white middle class population as the main consumer of cocaine has been well documented but was displaced from the national picture about the War on Drugs presented to the public by the media and government.

The coke factory sequence satirises such related societal anxieties in many ways, some of which are worth exploring further.

Primarily, the sequence fantasises about Reagan's impossible War on Drugs. RoboCop breaks down the door to the factory and then goes about singlehandedly annihilating the drug dealers, a crude metaphor of Reagan's extremist drug enforcement approach and typical of his moral crusades against the manufactured enemies of real America. The relative ease with which RoboCop enforces the War on Drugs (summed up symbolically in the shot of a test tube of cocaine, the glass crunching beneath the force of RoboCop's steel foot) pokes fun at the futility of Reagan's unrealistic policies, many of which were enacted simply for votes, but also acts out a sort of fantasy wish

Fig. 15. Arresting Boddicker in the coke factory

fulfilment, comparable to John Rambo's attempts to re-write America's defeat in the Vietnam War in *Rambo First Blood: Part II*.

The American economy in the 1980s thrived off drug culture. Yet what is subversive about the inhabitants of the coke factory in *RoboCop* is that they are mainly white. If we also consider the only people in the film shown to be taking taking cocaine are a white middle class yuppie and two prostitutes, this points to a parallel reality in the 1980s that the mainstream media often masked over. RoboCop shooting up a bunch of white guys is probably inconsequential to the bloodletting in the sequence but since Reagan's War on Drugs disproportionately targeted the black community, (while also positing that the drug trade as one controlled by white people may not be completely revolutionary), *RoboCop* does attempt to re-draw the ideological line, arguing the War on Drugs was a bi-racial phenomenon, and one in which many cases an impoverished white and black working class America was often the victim. If RoboCop is simply taking out the trash, there is a major disconnect when it comes Boddicker's alliance with OCP, the private corporate sphere, complicating the ethics of RoboCop's conduct in the coke factory. But even RoboCop's arrest of Boddicker is played out in the darkest of ways. In the DVD commentary on the Criterion release of the film, Verhoeven says it was ironic to have RoboCop throw Boddicker through the glass windows while reading him his rights since it provides an indictment of police behaviour and the incongruities of American society. The drug economy connection with corporate power resonates when Boddicker screams he has protection from OCP, an ideological sentiment that reiterates an earlier theme, that white-collar crime in Reagan America was a proxy mechanism.

While we are on the subject of white-collar villainy, Kurtwood Smith's turn as Clarence Boddicker is an inspired bit of casting. Since comic book fantasies are measured on the strength of the villain, Clarence Boddicker's repellent and 'icky'[31] sociopath is certainly a worthy opponent for RoboCop. Verhoeven has said Boddicker's neo-fascist look, the rimless, oval shaped bookish spectacles and the black/grey colour tones, was modelled on Heinrich Himmler. Smith succeeds in exuding a piquant mix of viciousness and charisma, ad-libbing many of the best lines, while Ronny Cox as Dick Jones defies audience expectations with a slimy role that defied his previously relatively placid star persona.

Boddicker, like Dick Jones is no ordinary villain. Foremost, he is a businessman. Upon entering the coke factory, Boddicker is negotiating with Sal, an obstinate cocaine manufacturer, the terms of a deal, and talks like someone in the corporate world: 'You want space in my marketplace? You're gonna have to give me a volume discount.' And when Sal downs turn Boddicker's initial cash offer, warning him off his notoriety as a cop killer, Boddicker refuses to back down: 'But I got the connections. I got the sales organisation.' The conquest of neoliberal values in Reagan's America, based on individualism, entrepreneurship, and the free market permeated all facets of American life, and in *RoboCop*'s vision of Detroit even the criminals have gained a legitimacy which is troubling to say the least.

Chapter 3: American Jesus

I began to see all sorts of social and philosophical elements. There are interesting ideas to do with reincarnation and the quest for a lost paradise. (1988 interview with Paul Verhoeven in Monthly Film Bulletin)

Having been massacred a second time, this time by his police brethren, a courageous Lewis rescues RoboCop. She takes RoboCop to the abandoned steel mill, indexical of a post-industrial age, and the grim locale for RoboCop's decisive confrontation with Boddicker. In some ways, the narrative comes full circle, falling back on itself in terms of locale, returning to the scene of Murphy's ferocious massacre. The wounded, dysfunctional robot, in this case a cyborg, now considered a threat to society, the same one he was asked to protect, is a complete reversal of the technological intent of the RoboCop program. And RoboCop's displacement to the steel mill, a haunting visual space, signifying the collapse of the first machine age, conjures a poignant affectation of the man-machine figure laid to waste.

More than ever, RoboCop's position as an outsider is cruelly emphasised in his pitiful, crumbling technological state. The bumbling empathy of Frankenstein's monster certainly comes to mind, and so does the poignant robotic imagery of Ted Hughes' The Iron Man, impressively translated in Brad Bird's underrated *The Iron Giant* film (1999). Decisively, RoboCop's decaying state explicates a markedly conventional statement, often inscribed in the science fiction genre, of the pace with which technology becomes obsolete. RoboCop's technological obsolescence can be read as a reaction to 'displacement and replication' (Seed, 2011: 60), which Seed argues, are 'two of the main fears in robot narratives' related to 'humans losing their centrality' (ibid.).

Though we recognise RoboCop's status as a cyborg, the visual explication of his hybrid status as a man-machine outsider only gains clarity towards the end of the film when RoboCop aversely removes his helmet, a sort of unmasking, concurrently forsaking and avowing his identity as a cyborg. This sequence will form the starting point of this chapter, exploring the film's portrayal of the cyborg, while discussing religious, philosophical and mythological dimensions, chiefly the potential of reading the film as an allegory of Christ. Whereas the Christ parable is nothing innovative to the way Hollywood heroism can be read, what makes *RoboCop's* Christian allegory markedly distinctive is it takes places in the context of the science fiction cyborg film sub-genre.

Cyber-culture

The term cyborg first coined in 1960 by Manfred Clynes and Nathan S. Kline is best described as a 'self-regulating man-machine system, supposed to be more flexible than the human organism thanks to the fusion of organic and mechanical parts' (Cavallaro, 2000: 45). Fusion, a distinctive marker of the cyborg, opines a synthesis or merging of identities often characterising the discombobulated state we find ourselves in with technology. Moreover, a technological fetishism has emerged in society, leading to a perversely ambivalent adoration of the outer and inner mechanics of technology. In 1927, Fritz Lang's *Metropolis* introduced us to the gynoid, a female robot, which is created at the behest of the industrialist so to subdue the workers revolt. In *Metropolis*, the maschinemensch ("machine-human") invented by Rotwang is not merely a decorative visual explication but channels an ideological potency that heralded a very early and influential politicisation of science fiction cinema. Thereafter the iconography of the robot developed exponentially.

In the 1960s and 1970s, science fiction literature visualised a litany of cyborgs. A significant feature of this corpus of speculative fiction was the consolidation of prosthesis as a key feature of the cyborg tale, which would gain wider cultural acceptance in the cyborg cinema of the 1980s in films such as *The Terminator*. *RoboCop* was part of this cycle of 1980 films in which the cyborg was consolidated as a genuinely ambivalent iconographic motif of science fiction cinema. And yet, Springer argues 'the terms robot, android, and cyborg generate a great deal of confusion and are sometimes mistakenly interchanged. It is only the cyborg, however, that represents the fusion of particular human beings with technology' (Springer, 1996: 20). Indeed, Springer attempts to differentiate between the three terms (RoboCop's cyborg status is complicated by his hulking outer body armour) explicating the iconographic identity of a robot. But it is only when RoboCop finally removes his helmet does his cyborg identity become plain to see.

The cyborg was specifically communicative of the cyberpunk sub-culture, which emerged in the late 1980s and early 1990s. Springer writes: 'Popular culture has probed the implications of technological fusion most consistently in the sub-genre of science fiction called cyberpunk' (Springer, 1996: 31). It might be promising to make a case for *RoboCop* as a cyberpunk film but since it is rarely referred to in such terms this label understandably reflects the film's complicated genre status. But *RoboCop* certainly is a cyberpunk film in the dystopian imaginings of Detroit and particularly in the 'terminal identity' label coined by Scott Bukataman and which Springer defines as 'the integration of humans with computers and the cessation of human life as we know it' (Springer, 1996: 44).

The integration between man and machine is realised in the ways in which RoboCop's system is rigorously controlled by technology, even when he sleeps. Cavallaro argues 'the virtual interchangability of human bodies and machines is a recurring theme in cyberpunk' (Cavallaro, 2000: 12). This blurring of boundaries between man and machine has produced 'one of the prevailing figurations in a culture dominated by science and technology' (Smelik, 2010: 14), a complicated technological paradigm that reached a theological zenith with Donna Haraway's 'Manifesto for Cyborgs' in 1984.

Haraway's theorisation of cyborg politics was a 'response to a call for political thinking about the 1980s from socialist-feminist points of view (Haraway, 1984: 190), and much of her work re-thought the figure of the cyborg as an apolitical entity, a purist idea that transcends racial and gender boundaries that habitually define capitalist society. Sean Redmond argues there are two types of cyborg that populate the science fiction universe: 'humanist – driven by the logic of the machine aesthetic and longs for the human attachment' and the 'pathological' that 'wants nothing more than the complete genocide of the human race' (Redmond, 2004: 156). Whereas *The Terminator* falls into the latter and the pathological cyborg is commonly found in the cyborg film sub-genre, *RoboCop* clearly conforms to the ideal of the humanist cyborg and works through this longing for human attachment via the theme of memories.

Unmasking the Cyborg

Some of the aforementioned ideas will be explored further, analysing the unmasking sequence from the film, which occurs at the steelworks. This unmasking comes after RoboCop has been pushed into a sort of technological exile, signified by his ostracism from the police force. The sequence begins with Lewis returning to the steelworks from the police precinct, telling us that it was deserted because of the strike. Lewis finds RoboCop struggling to reset his leg as a consequence of the physical damage inflicted on his body armour by the police. As Smelik argues, 'Another visual topos in cyborg films is to systematically destroy the cyborg so as to repair it' (Smelik, 2010: 93), denoting regeneration as a key trait in the cyborg tale. The destruction and resurrection of the cyborg is a narrative trope inherent in the repeated attacks RoboCop comes under from OCP, the police force, Boddicker and Dick Jones. By the time RoboCop strolls into OCP at the end, it is astonishing he is still functioning. Lewis tells RoboCop what she has brought back with her. This includes his gun, a drill and some baby food. And as RoboCop begins to drill into both sides of his helmet, something sacred is about to revealed. Before he removes the helmet, RoboCop pauses, saying: 'You may not like what you're going to see.' This warning to Lewis, and also to the audience, is an unmasking that recalls the horror idioms. Traditionally the unmasking in a horror film is staged melodramatically whereby we come face to face with the monstrous dread that has been lingering over the narrative, but this fastidious unveiling in *RoboCop* is a desolate and melancholic imagining. Indeed, the pathos of Peter Weller recalls Boris Karloff's lasting performance as Frankenstein's monster. This humanisation of RoboCop in the final third of the film's narrative is critical in terms of determining the shifting emotional response of the audience.

When RoboCop removes the helmet, the camera position shifts to the back of his head, denying us an objectifying and grandiose close up. The denial of a major reveal is withheld temporarily. Instead we are shown the grotesque artificial machinery of Security Concepts melding with the real flesh of Murphy, conveying a disturbing image of cyborg technology. Beneath the shiny, muscular titanium conceit is something dreadfully human. The unearthly merging of flesh and steel leaves a cold register in the gaze of the audience, framing the corporate engineering of Security

Fig. 16. RoboCop - unmasking

Concepts as a heinous transgression. When Lewis holds up a makeshift mirror, RoboCop can finally look upon the human face of Murphy; 'the technological double' (Telotte, 1994: 234). In the uneven mirror Murphy's reflection is contorted, a ghostly projection of the past, but clearly invoking a doubling or 'uncanny reflection of the self' (Correa, 2007: 125). On the soundtrack, the haunting memories leitmotif, used emotively in the 'going home' sequence, projects a troubling ambience.

J. P. Telotte argues the film works through postmodern anxieties of the doppelgänger, in the form of the cyborg, re-connecting to the wider existential crisis that has been leading up to this critical moment. But Telotte sees this doubling crisis resolve itself in the 'triumph of the self' (Telotte, 1994: 244) when RoboCop reclaims his human identity at the end:

> What RoboCop reveals is how the human, at least that in which we typically think of the human as residing, our consciousness, can endure despite what seems to be our every, unthinking effort to eradicate all trace of it. (Telotte, 1994: 244)

As I have previously discussed the corporation is unable to comprehend that it cannot completely eradicate the human identity of Murphy; traces remain, a ghostly residue. RoboCop's delicate inspection of his human flesh, with his metal fingers caressing the soft skin, indicates strangeness to the unmasking. Smelik writes: 'Such reparation scenes excel in ambiguity because the once-unbeatable machine has become defenceless flesh' (Smelik, 2010: 93). But the flesh of RoboCop is not as defenceless as Smelik assigns to the cyborg; it is very much alive and responsive to a past trauma with which RoboCop has yet to reconcile.

The next shot cuts to a medium close up of RoboCop as he continues looking in the mirror. What becomes apparent from this shot is the childlike image we are presented of RoboCop. His baby face explicates an intensely disabling sagacity of vulnerability, exposed by a brutal nakedness. RoboCop's helplessness is heightened by his pictorial isolation within the sequence when a master shot is later deployed to extenuate his servile loneliness. The cinematographic choice of loose framing, isolating RoboCop in the wretched post-industrial milieu, is magnified by the haunting musical motif resurfacing on the soundtrack and restating an ethereal tendency. The bullet wound, still visible, a totem of Boddicker's monstrosity and relation to Murphy's human past, augments the peculiarity of his man-machine self.

In some ways, the unmasking also signals the point at which RoboCop stops becoming a cyborg. In his 1987 review, critic Roger Ebert, who always expressed an unparalleled fondness for American genre cinema, attests 'a lot of RoboCop's personality is expressed by his voice, which is a mechanical monotone', a salient observation by Ebert magnifying a minutiae that often go unnoticed in the film. The unvaried, exacting monotone which acts as an aural marker of RoboCop's cyborg identity is replaced by one familiar to us, the unmistakably illogical, hesitant voice of a human. And when Lewis says 'It's really good to see you again, Murphy', she does with some elation. But RoboCop does not share her enthusiasm, enquiring on the whereabouts of his wife and son. Alternatively, the unmasking can be read as liberation for RoboCop since it sets him of on a journey to reclaim his identity, but precariously as a vigilante. Manaugh writes the cyborg is 'like the Japanese notion of Tsukumogami, that is, self aware material objects that manage to wake up, possessed by an intelligent spirit' (Manaugh, 2014). One could argue there is an awakening of the soul once thought dead, an idea that runs through the 'going home' sequence; the spectral self that haunts the body.

When Lewis tells RoboCop his wife and son moved away and started over again, he listens, paralysed by the verity of the life he once had. RoboCop responds poignantly, 'I can feel them. But I can't remember them.' The cyborg's faculty to emote and communicate human feelings is unremittingly attractive for science fiction writers, and has become a classic trope in cyborg cinema. For example, in *Terminator 2: Judgement Day* (1992), Arnold Schwarzenegger's pathological cyborg is reimagined as an empathetic altruistic surrogate father. This shift in the representation of the cyborg over the course of the first two Terminator films was also indirectly in accordance to the way science fiction cinema in the early 1990s was deploying narratives in which the father once destabilised from the genre re-emerged to be consolidated as part of the family unit: '*Star Wars* and *Close Encounters* present us with a picture of disintegrating family structures and absentee fathers, a feature that became common in science fiction films that followed in the early 1980s' (Cornea, 2007: 114). Decisively, the unmasking sequence ends with RoboCop telling Lewis he wants to be left alone, a sense of loss washing over him.

The affecting response in the closing moment of the unmasking sequence evidences RoboCop is a humanist cyborg, exhibiting an emotional maturity that makes us want to empathise with his predicament. But what should we make of his revelatory thoughts on his wife and son: 'I can feel them. But I can't remember them'? RoboCop says he cannot remember his wife and son, but as we recognise from the coming home sequence, he does remember. However, what he does recall are merely fragments of a life. And since RoboCop has been unmasked now, and will remain so throughout the rest of the film, the human identity of Murphy takes over and asserts itself more spiritedly. In this context, as Murphy, the human self, he cannot remember in the way the technology that controls his system as RoboCop has done for him in the past. Since this is Murphy speaking now, the assertion that he can 'feel them' is a haunting one, suggesting an ethereal connection and eternal bond that remains un-severed.

Transmigration and gender identities

In many ways, it is the complicated experience of emotion and memory that defines the ubiquity of the cyborg in science fiction cinema. Referring to the 'transmigration' theory of Robotics professor Hans Moravec, who helped pioneer the development of Artificial Intelligence (A.I.), Springer writes that Moravec 'describes how someday it will be possible for human mental functions to be organically extracted from the human brain and transferred to computer software' (Springer, 1996: 29). And what about memories? Can they replicated or preserved? The role of memories in the cyborg figure seems to be a wider metaphysical question the film poses, taken up powerfully in *Blade Runner*, with regards to the trans-migratory experience of *RoboCop*, questioning the legitimacy of positing the transformation of Murphy to RoboCop as a post-human concept. Unlike the robot or android, both technological simulacra, the cyborg's tentative connection to humanity is what makes RoboCop's internal struggle over his true identity so compelling; the fusion is complete but the unending mysteries of the human soul remain unanswered. And if the punk in cyberpunk was fashionably appropriated as a measure of ideological resistance then such a euphemism certainly manifests itself in RoboCop's refusal to become fully assimilated into the corporate system, rendering him an outsider. Not everyone is in agreement though about cyberpunk's 'revolutionary potential' (Schaub, 2001: 81). Writing in 2001, and referring predominately to the work of Nicola Nixon, Joseph Schaub argues cyberpunk was a 'reactionary movement attempting to undermine the efforts of Utopian feminist SF writers of the 1970s, such as Joanna Russ and Ursula K. LeGuin' (ibid.). This reactionary determination in terms of gender politics is equivalent to the ways in which the sub-genre of the slasher film and the ubiquitous final girl trope has been seen as a reaction to the gains of the 1970s feminist movement.

Springer claims 'sexual identity is not entirely rigid in cyberpunk texts' (Springer, 1996: 64), which is often the case in cyberpunk cinema. *RoboCop* doesn't necessarily broach sexual and gender identity but as I discussed in an earlier chapter, the idea of masculinity in crisis is one that emerges in the context of a Western film genre reading of the traditional constructions of masculinity. Springer suggests the cyborg is often a site of contestation for sexuality: 'steely hard phallic strength is opposed to feminine fluidity' (Springer, 1996: 103). To become RoboCop Murphy undergoes 'total body prosthesis', at the insistence of Bob Morton, which we assume includes the removal of his penis. Both Morton and Boddicker enact this process of emasculation, via a form of symbolic castration, but in different ways. Whereas Boddicker obliterates

Murphy's gun-hand, Morton resorts to technology to finish the castration, a totalising annihilation of Murphy's male body.

If the cyborg is typically presented as an androgynous creature, and although Murphy has been neutered so to speak, why is it that he can still feel sexual desire? In the 'going home' sequence, one of the flashback memories that RoboCop recalls is of his wife, smiling seductively in the bedroom, reminding us of his happy sex life. In some ways, the desire remains for affection and also for sex. Perhaps much wider is a companionship RoboCop seeks. Such attributes seem to be etched into the human subconscious. A common theme in cyberpunk culture is 'jacking in' whereby 'the act of interfacing with a computer matrix is...a sexual act' (Springer, 1996: 68), which Springer also labels as a 'masturbatory fantasy' (ibid.). A phallic metal spike RoboCop uses to jack in to the computer system can be inferred as a substitute for Murphy's lack of a penis. Ironically, the metal spike, a technological attachment enabling RoboCop to discover the identity of Boddicker and his assailants is inverted at the end. In the final gory confrontation between RoboCop and Boddicker, RoboCop inadvertently transforms the spike into an agent of death, recording a sexual release. If the metal spike stands in for the lack of a penis, then psychologically, RoboCop impales Boddicker with his penis, thereby producing a homoerotic frisson to this denouement and reiterating the contestation of sexual identity performed in the film.

Mecha-anime

Japanese Mecha-anime, with which the film shares a number of traits, first appeared in the 1960s on Japanese television. The international success of *Astro Boy* in 1963 heralded a long line of anime involving humanistic robots. Unlike science fiction films featuring cyborgs Mecha-anime are darker and more violent. Susan Napier writes:

> While the imagery in mecha anime is strongly technological and is often specifically focused on the machinery of the armoured body, the narratives themselves often focus to a surprising extent on the human inside the machinery. (Napier, 2004: 205)

Mecha's emphasis on interiority bears some parallels with RoboCop's repeated concerns with exploring the identity of Murphy/RoboCop through a metaphysical prism. In her discussion of Mecha-anime, Napier refers to three anime, two of which were made in the late 1980s, around about the same time as *RoboCop*. While *RoboCop* is rarely ever associated with Mecha-anime, there are conventions the film borrows from Mecha-anime, further complicating RoboCop's genre status. One convention in particular, as noted by Napier – 'virtually any mecha narrative will build up to lengthy climactic fight between huge and powerful machines engaged in combat involving crushing, dismemberment and explosions' (Napier, 2004: 206) – is tangibly suggested through the brawl amongst RoboCop and ED-209 in OCP HQ.

In the brawl, ED-209's attempt to annihilate RoboCop is met with unexpected resistance. While this brawl acts out a perverse fantasy to do with the unchecked masculine power of corporate executives, it is the 'exaltation of the augmented body...around which mecha plots revolve' (Napier, 2004: 207). At one point in the brawl, RoboCop's eye under his helmet becomes exposed, pointing not only to the human interiority of Murphy, but depicting 'the technologically armoured body with profound ambivalence' (Napier, 2004: 205). But the film's ambivalence to body politics is far from simply evoking Mecha-anime, since body politics is an abiding theme in the American films of Paul Verhoeven. Characters struggling to retain a physical and ideological ownership over their bodies act as thematic glue in Verhoeven's American films, particularly his loose trilogy of science fiction films. As Cavallaro argues:

Cyberculture pivots on a contradiction: a growing fascination with the body, testified by all sorts of media, coexists with an increasing infiltration of the body by technologies that seem to take its materiality away. (Cavallaro, 2000: 75)

RoboCop is perhaps more Mecha than a lot of its contemporaries from the 1980s era of science fiction cinema but it is a tentative argument which needs developing further especially in relation to the ubiquity of the cyborg in popular culture.

RoboCop as Christian allegory

Shifting from a discussion of the cyborg to Christ seems a little jarring to say the least but since we are dealing with materiality, bodies and the metaphysical, religious sentiments seem altogether probable. This next part of the chapter deals with reading RoboCop as a Jesus metaphor, an elucidation put forward most fervently by Paul Verhoeven. Throughout the 1990s Verhoeven harboured a dream of making an epic film project on Jesus but sadly was never given the green light, most probably because of the likely controversy a project of this nature would instigate.[32] In 2010 Verhoeven, also a member of The Jesus Seminar,[33] published *Jesus of Nazareth*,[34] his personal interpretation of the story of Jesus. Director Paul Schrader, reviewing the book for Film Comment, argues Verhoeven draws a number of contentious inferences about Jesus. Perhaps the most provocative is Verhoeven's claim that 'Jesus was a firebrand and a revolutionary (some would say "terrorist")' (Schrader, 2010: 76). Verhoeven's fascination with the contested narrative space of Jesus's life is divisive. But what does this mean for the ways in which the figure of RoboCop has been talked about in popular discourse?

It seems unforgivable to make the dreaded assumption that heroism implicit in Hollywood action cinema can in fact be interpreted as an allegory of both Jesus and Christ. While the role of religious iconography has been over-determined in Hollywood cinema, the Christ-figure has been a constant source of attraction that stretches back to the Hollywood studio era evident across many film genres. Over time the dominant representation of a martyred/crucified Christ has become part of the visual repository of Hollywood cinema, unequivocally rendered a terrible, overwrought cliché. *Rocky* anyone? But how broadly can the argument of reading RoboCop as a Christ-figure be sustained? This demands a closer look at the characterisation of RoboCop/Murphy in relation to the structure of the narrative.

RoboCop as a Christ-figure

Peter Malone says we need to make a distinction between the Jesus-figure and the Christ-figure: 'The Jesus-figure is any representation of himself' while 'the Christ-figure is a character (from history, fiction, visual arts, poetry, drama, music, cinema) who is presented as resembling Jesus in a significant way' (Malone, 2012: 12). In this regard RoboCop resembles a Christ-figure. But to what extent is this indicative in the construction of the narrative? Verhoeven has pointed to moments where the Christian allegorising is overtly manifested through the symbolism. This includes the massacre of Murphy, the resurrection of Murphy as RoboCop, and the often talked about walking on water moment towards the end of the film. While it would be sufficient to centre on these particular moments, scholar Lloyd Baugh 'proposes a list of eight criteria for identifying cinematic Christ-figures' (Reinhartz, 2013: 151), a useful framework for further analysis. Baugh's criteria includes:

(1) Mysterious origins, (2) charisma (the ability to attract followers), (3) a commitment to justice, (4) withdraw to a deserted place, (5) become embroiled in conflict with authorities, (6) provide redemption for others, (7) suffer, and (8) achieve post-death recognition. (Reinhartz, 2013: 151)

Determining suitable criteria with which to identify Christ-figures in film, Reinhartz also refers to the work of Anton Kozlovic. Kozlovic contends science fiction cinema has consistently acted as an ideal vehicle for Biblical stories. In this regard Kozlovic's work is more pertinent than Baugh's, arguing the Christ-figure in the form of a 'benign entity' (Kozlovic, 2004: 26) has characterised many popular science fiction films including '*The Day The Earth Stood Still, E.T., Starman, The Matrix*' (ibid.) to name a few. Mapping Baugh's criteria onto the film's narrative may help to clarify the extent to which RoboCop/Murphy is a Christ-figure.

Baugh's initial criteria, 'mysterious origins', appear problematic but Murphy's introduction could be viewed as enigmatic since there is no backstory. Kozlovic says Christ-figures are 'usually outsiders of their communities' (ibid.), and Murphy as the stranger who arrives at a new police precinct certainly preys on the idea of the outsider. Furthermore, Murphy feels that if he is to belong to a new police community he must prove his worth, an action that tragically backfires. Murphy's outsider status is later amplified when RoboCop is ostracised by the police force, retreating to the steel mill. Given the status of RoboCop/Murphy as a figure of law enforcement, 'a commitment to justice' characterises pretty much all of the crime genre.

Reading RoboCop as a Christ figure along the lines of Kozlovic and Baugh may feel like a prescriptive exercise as it can only point to a structuralism and miss the perversity of Verhoeven's seditious vision of Jesus's story. Also, a religiously coded RoboCop points to a conservatism clashing with the cynicism of a bleak dystopian imagining. A prescriptive, conservative reading puts in jeopardy all that makes RoboCop a genuinely disruptive and ambivalent societal force. Verhoeven's Christ as projected through RoboCop is a rose in the gutter, a knight in shining armour, the messiah in a world gone to shit.

As discussed earlier, Murphy's commitment to justice and his eagerness to prove his worth as a self-righteous lawman initially results in a fatal confrontation with Boddicker and his goons. Murphy's death is a brutal one, articulated visually through the iconology of crucifixion, a potent signifier of Christ. The first image of crucifixion is when Boddicker shoots Murphy's gun hand. The overhead shot extenuates the religious significance of this graphic allusion, depicting the outstretched arms of Murphy on the ground in a crucified pose. When the goons eviscerate Murphy, he raises his arms into the air, and a slight allusion to crucifixion is reiterated. But more than crucifixion is the suffering Murphy undergoes in this agonising moment, a suffering he also endures as RoboCop when his police brethren are instructed to kill him. Undeniably, resurrection is the deepest link to thinking of RoboCop as a Christ figure. Murphy's rising from the dead is not a miracle in the religious sense but a technological one instigated by the new gods of society – the corporate capitalists. This equivocation complicates attempts to read RoboCop as a Messiah figure because although he does appear as a liberator, rescuing innocent citizens from the dregs of a cancerous society, RoboCop is ultimately a corporate puppet. Read alternatively, OCP's indirect creation of a Messiah in the figure of RoboCop is another form of demagoguery, appealing to the primal sentiments of a disillusioned, hopeless society, but with the subdued political intention of both distracting and misleading the public.

Oddly enough RoboCop has to be liberated first by his partner Lewis who in terms of Biblical discourse occupies a redemptive role herself. While it would not be possible to compare Lewis to Mary Magdalene, she is perhaps closest to John the Baptist since she helps RoboCop to liberate himself from the tyranny of the corporate masters, realising his potential as a skewed Messiah. But how do we reconcile RoboCop as a vigilante with the Christ-figure who believed in forgiveness? Kozlovic's (2001) analysis of four science fiction films refers to the cyborg-messiah/saviour in *Terminator 2*. RoboCop is no messiah or a saviour since he is driven by revenge, adopting the guise of a vigilante. Neither does RoboCop forgive his killers, an altruistic feature archetypally associated with the Christ-figure. After RoboCop discovers the truth about his past, he sets on a revenge mission and his commitment to justice becomes displaced. An analysis of this confrontation will be the focus of the next part of this chapter, considering how the representation of RoboCop as a subversive Christ-figure fits in with Verhoeven's personal interpretation of Jesus.

'Looking for me?' – Subverting the Christ-figure

A wide angle shot frames Boddicker and his clan, armed with newly acquired military style guns from Dick Jones, nervously marching through the steel mill searching for RoboCop with the hope of killing him. RoboCop throws a piece of metal catching their attention. Startled, they begin firing erratically, creating a series of explosions which comes to nothing. Suddenly from above RoboCop, a reinvigorated force, cries 'Looking for me?' As the gang turn to look up to see where RoboCop is, he shoots repeatedly at Joe, killing him. Since Boddicker and his goons are terrifyingly lawless and operate with no ethical code whatsoever, it presents a moral justification for RoboCop to act comparably. But this is the first time in the narrative when RoboCop disregards the prime directives[35] and he does after having unmasked, discarding the identity bestowed upon by OCP. Obviously, Jesus would never have condoned such vigilantism but in Verhoeven's purview RoboCop's reincarnation as a Christ-figure is a modernist, perverse depiction. By killing Joe, a transgression occurs in which RoboCop's amoral actions equates him with Boddicker. This recalls an uneasy trope of the crime film, as suggested dubiously by the iconic character of Harry Callaghan (Clint Eastwood) in the Dirty Harry films, in which the detective has to transgress the law to paradoxically restore social order. But this ultimately means RoboCop crosses a moral and political threshold that cannot lawfully sanction his vengeful act. Emil, Leon and Boddicker retaliate, firing at RoboCop, but he walks away unscathed, and in a stirring image of defiance and beauty, there is a medium close up of RoboCop glancing down at his perpetrators framed by the smoke and sparks from the explosions, visualising an exhibition of valour.

As Emil and Boddicker race ahead to cut off RoboCop, Leon pursues RoboCop on foot, firing repeatedly but missing each time. In the melee, RoboCop comes away unscathed, laconically strutting away from the explosions, projecting a strength that not only reiterates his superiority as a cyborg but also hinting at a Christ-like invulnerability. As RoboCop outsmarts Boddicker and his goons, the 'RoboCop theme' peaks again. Emil's fate is the most grotesque. He spots RoboCop and speeds up so he can run him over but RoboCop fires at the windscreen, shattering it, thereby making it difficult for Emil to see. Next, RoboCop coolly turns and walks away just as Emil crashes his van into toxic waste. The doors to the back of the van open, toxic waste flooding out. Emil emerges, his skin hanging of his bones, a deformed human sick bag that hobbles away in agony. Leon is repulsed by Emil and pushes him away. In a brief but intense car chase Lewis pursues Boddicker through the steel mill. Unable to brake in time, Emil is literally splattered across Boddicker's windscreen. Consequently, Boddicker loses control; the car flips, landing in a murky pool of water below the main steelworks. Lewis gets out of her patrol car to check if Boddicker is dead. But before Lewis can react, Boddicker begins firing indiscriminately. Lewis, fatally wounded, rolls down the embankment, falling into the pool. The speed with which the action unfolds in this sequence is edited with a chaotic rhythm, creating a befitting apocalyptic spectacle in which a primal confrontation between good and evil comes to the fore; the aesthetic, thematic tenor reaches a biblical explication.

Boddicker prepares to finish off Lewis. Framed in a dynamic asymmetrically composed shot, Boddicker raises his gun, sarcastically uttering 'Bye-bye, Baby!' repeating the now familiar juxtaposition of violence and comedy. Boddicker's face is a mess; the shattered glass in his spectacles and streaks of blood running across his face reiterates an implacable monstrosity. In the context of a Christian allegory, Boddicker's refusal to die and his continuous indomitability create a demonic affectation. But who is bold enough to take on this personification of evil? Why Verhoeven's American Jesus of course! Dramatically, off screen we hear RoboCop exclaiming 'Clarence!' Boddicker takes heed and looks on in astonishment at RoboCop, miraculously striding across the pool of water and 'filmed as if he were walking on water toward Clarence, the man who had "crucified" him' (Keesey, 2005: 106). Verhoeven's realisation of an American Jesus is codified explicitly with this deliberate allusion to Christian mythology, imbuing the spectacle with Biblical overtones. Speaking on the DVD commentary for the film Verhoeven says:

> Religion has really lost its non-aggressive attitude that was originally proposed by Jesus, and has come to be part of a political system where people think that they do good and they do the wish of God when they kill the other people.

Fig. 17 Walking on water

The implication that religion, once an autonomous body of thought, has been co-opted into politics is a troubling phenomenon for Verhoeven. American Presidents have continually taken political decisions based on religious sentiments and beliefs (and as have UK politicians, such as Tony Blair), invading countries in the name of God (George Bush Jr.) and then justifying the cost of human life as motivated by an inexplicable Christian morality. In this instance the Jesus Verhoeven conjures is a definitely fascist one. 'I'm not arresting you anymore,' exclaims RoboCop as he moves towards Boddicker. Verhoeven says:

> He has done with Clarence, the time of turning the other cheek is over. Americans want to be humane, but if they think it takes too long, Christian morality is

pushed aside for the moment and they go for their weapon – just like RoboCop. (Verhoeven, 1997: 229)

While Verhoeven argues there is an abandonment of Christian morality in RoboCop's pursuit of Boddicker, this sentiment is contradicted by explicating the walking on water miracle supposedly performed by Jesus. Verhoeven's American Jesus is a deeply contradictory imagining, a schizophrenic reflection of the American psyche and its interminable relationship with Christianity.

The acutely drawn observations of America Verhoeven paints in his Hollywood films centre predominately on the representations of violence, power and gender. The outsider's gaze he brought to American genre cinema in the 1980s and 1990s probed thematic contradictions with fresh eyes, unveiling aspects of the American psyche invisible to most filmmakers. When Verhoeven talks of Americans 'going for their weapon' when 'they think it takes too long' is in fact a commentary on contemporary imperialistic endeavours, proselytising a notion of foreign policy shaped through coercion, intervention and down the barrel of a gun. Furthermore, the reversion to violence and guns as a means of resolution still rings true today, plaguing the ways in which gun-related violence has become a casual reflex action, altogether present in the private and public sphere of American life.

Interminable resurrection

As I have previously stated the crumbling post-industrial facade of the steelworks is a fitting backdrop to RoboCop's frail state. But the milieu also functions vividly as a bleak landscape to the biblical tone struck by the apocryphal clash. The brown, murky water, the twisted pieces of metal, the harshness of the concrete, conjure a putrid, repulsive urban milieu. Unwarily RoboCop moves towards Boddicker, failing to realise Leon has taken control of a hydraulic crane, positioning a chunk of scrap metal over RoboCop with the intention of killing him. Simultaneously, Lewis crawls to Boddicker's gun. Leon drops the metal directly onto RoboCop, crushing him. As Boddicker celebrates with Leon, Lewis shoots up at Leon, killing him in a deadly fireball explosion. Enraged, Boddicker rushes over to RoboCop, who is trapped in the wreckage.

Although RoboCop is a machine, the repeated emphasis on his invincibility and refusal to die implies a perpetual state of renewal. A savage Boddicker repeatedly hits RoboCop with a metal spear, finally piercing the armour and drilling the spear into RoboCop. The symbolism of the piercing of RoboCop finds a comparative equivocation in the imagery of crucifixion, the spear coming to stand in for the nails used to crucify Christ. The mayhem of this epic contestation is extenuated through the imagery of fire that now litters the *mise-en-scène*, an impression of hell. It is worth noting the 'staking' of RoboCop invokes vampire iconography, returning the film to its horror antecedents, suitably deployed at a dreadful axis.

And when Boddicker stakes RoboCop, RoboCop lets out an unholy cry that is magnified through editing, cutting to a close up, depicting the indescribable pain. Apparent here again is the anguish RoboCop endures, invoking the interminable suffering of Christ. As Boddicker readies to kill RoboCop, RoboCop surprises Boddicker with his metal spike, wounding Boddicker fatally in the neck/throat, severing his arteries. Boddicker's death is a macabre and gruesome sight, embodied in the gory image of RoboCop drenched in Boddicker's blood. Boddicker is slaughtered like a feral animal, holding in vain his severed arteries, finally falling down dead into the pool of water. The slaying of Boddicker returns to the horror genre since Boddicker's gruesome death is framed in terms of the monster's defeat, a classic horror trope. And while RoboCop's quest for revenge is fulfilled, the contradiction with Christian morality ultimately makes Verhoeven's American Jesus perversely ambiguous.

With the death of Boddicker, RoboCop's bloodlust is satiated, but the price of retribution is a wounded partner and a distortion of justice. While RoboCop allots justice with a reversion to violence, his vigilantism takes place within neither the public or private sphere; it occurs in the realms of a post-industrial wasteland, personalising revenge. Nonetheless, RoboCop's vigilantism does not go unchecked; it is reined back in when he achieves 'post-death recognition', another of Baugh's criteria used to determine the Christ-figure in films. This 'post-death recognition' comes at the end when RoboCop refers to himself as Murphy, but the dubious corroboration of RoboCop's brutal slaying of Dick Jones reinforces the contemporary perversion of the Christ-figure. And with the thumbs up from the corporate lackeys, RoboCop's corporate resurrection is a zenith that seems him transformed into a cyborg-saviour, offering salvation, not to the people, but to his corporate masters. The bottom line is Verhoeven's American Jesus is an interminable demarcation of the toxic interactions of politics, religion and violence that define the complicated, incongruous yet endlessly captivating psyche of America.

Chapter 4: The Legacy of *RoboCop*

Released in the summer season of 1987, *RoboCop* was an unexpected commercial success, leading to the creation of the *RoboCop* universe, extending into television, video games, animation and numerous sequels. This final chapter is a short one and deals with legacy of *RoboCop* in terms of the original critical reception, the film's relationship with its two sequels, the marketing of the film and a brief consideration of Verhoeven's work in the Hollywood science fiction genre.

Critical Responses

In the US, *RoboCop* received an X rating when it was submitted to the MPAA and later re-cut for an R rating so it could be released in cinemas. Verhoeven had already established a reputation for sex and violence in European cinema, major themes in his Dutch films, and combined with the film's initial X rating, *RoboCop* built up somewhat of a controversial reputation before US critics could pass judgement.

In 1987 *RoboCop* was met with a mixed critical reception. US critics including Roger Ebert (New York Post), Walter Goodman (New York Times), Michael Willmington (Los Angeles Times) and David Denby (New York Magazine) gave a partially favourable response to the film, praising the satirical politics including the corporate allegorising and the post-human crisis: 'At its best, *RoboCop* makes something resonant and funny out of that standard science-fiction trauma – the mechanization of the human, the humanization of the automatic' (Denby, 1987: 58). Many of the favourable reviews were still critical of the film's use of violence, pointing to the widening role of exploitation in 1980s genre cinema: 'Part of what action movies have been doing in the last dozen years or so is discovering a way of releasing the audience from the normal "moral" responses to death' (ibid.). Denby goes onto (unfairly) suggest *RoboCop* is a bricolage of other American action and science fiction films, arguing Verhoeven's creative talents as a reputed European filmmaker are not given enough opportunity to flourish. But when the film was released in the UK in 1988, critics including notably Philip Strick (Monthly Fill Bulletin), one of the best writers on science fiction cinema, Hilary Mantel (The Spectator) and Judith Williamson (New

Statesman) responded in a far more positive way, singling out the subversive tone for a what was an unconventional mainstream genre film. British film critics offered a far more sophisticated critique, debating the violence in the film, a point taken up by Hilary Mantel:

> Wimpish critics are muttering about the scene where Murphy – the human Murphy – is comprehensively shot; but you have seen worse in Vietnam films. Their violence is excused because of the directors' intentions, which are often impeccably liberal; but these intentions seldom cut much ice with the ordinary cinema audience, who drool – if drooling is their bent – just the same. (Mantel, 1988: 260)

Mantel argues directors can often use the guise of political sentiments when it comes to depicting violence and critics/audiences respond accordingly. Verhoeven really got it in the neck for his supposed depictions of ultra violence and while the cloak of liberalism can often be enough to render criticisms regarding violence irrelevant, genre cinema especially science fiction and horror, often considered to be part of low culture, is an easy target for critical and artistic vilification. The largely appreciative, sophisticated cultural response from British critics to *RoboCop*'s nuances and ambiguities can be explained in terms of the empathy shown with Verhoeven's position as an outsider, looking at America through a European gaze.

There were a considerable slew of critics in the US who responded indifferently to *RoboCop*. This included Julie Salamon (Wall Street Journal), David Sterritt (Christian Science Monitor), Pauline Kael (New Yorker) and Dave Kehr (Chicago Tribune), condemning the film for its nastiness, cynicism and graphic violence. Kehr criticised the film's cheap juxtaposition of violence and sarcasm, which he argued was imported from Schwarzenegger's films, resulting in uneven results: 'The effect may or may not be a pernicious one, but it is certainly mechanical and certainly underhanded – another way for movies to prey on reflexive responses, a further extension of the ancient low road' (Kehr, 1987).

Much of the negative criticism focused on the representation of violence, questioning the intentions of the director and those involved. In fact, the over-determination of violence would become a defining bone of contention in the reception of most of

Verhoeven's American films, often displacing the deeper ideological themes at work. While the emphasis on sex and violence was a hangover from Verhoeven's European reputation, much of the initial critical reception failed to engage with the film's status as a science fiction film, instead framing *RoboCop* as an action film, which is some ways was more palatable for a summer blockbuster crowd.

RoboCop's mixed critical reception was a trend that plagued many of the best science fiction films of the 1980s. Problematic science fiction films with darker metaphysical aspirations, such as *Blade Runner, The Thing* (1982) and *Starman* (1984), were often incompatible with the more romantic, sentimental science fiction works like *E.T.,* *Star Wars*, and *Close Encounters of the Third Kind*. It is not without reason why many of overlooked 1980s science fiction films have been reclaimed over the years by film culture. Since *RoboCop* was a commercial success and thus co-opted by default into the mainstream canon of science fiction cinema, the film's critical reputation was salvaged most expressly by the authorial currency of Verhoeven. *RoboCop* was surprisingly well marketed by Orion pictures and the respective merchandising opportunities helped to create a specific iconography around the figure of RoboCop in popular culture. Unlike the commercial failures of *Blade Runner* and *The Thing*, two of the best science fiction films of the 1980s, *RoboCop*'s box office success was unusual in this respect, following in the line of *The Terminator*, marking it as a key breakout film for the evolution of the cyborg sub-genre and cyberpunk cinema.

Reclaiming *RoboCop*

Given the film's astounding commercial success and mainstream audience acceptance, it almost became necessary to re-claim the work from the realms of populism and re-assert its ideological complexities. And the first major cultural reading of *RoboCop* appeared in 1989 in the journal Jump Cut. There were two pieces; the first by Julie Codell titled 'Murphy's Law, RoboCop's body and Capitalism's work' and the second by Steven Best, 'In the detrius of technology'. Both Codell and Best analysed the film as a substantial text, undertaking a Marxist reading of the film's critique of capitalism lurking beneath the action/science fiction conventions:

> The ultimate irony in the film is that applying Marx's hope that the workers' bodies can be protected, extended, expanded through their labors' products, Americans live in a world in which we, the only workers of the world who can reap the benefits by consuming mass quantities, reap only the benefits of destruction by malfunction. And the destruction is total. (Codell, 1989: 19)

In the late 1990s, The Criterion Collection, a boutique home video label specialising in the distribution of cult, classic and contemporary international cinema, released an unrated director's cut of *RoboCop*, first on Laserdisc and later DVD. Criterion's boutique release certainly cemented the status of *RoboCop* as a cult film but more importantly canonised the work as essential to 1980s American cinema. The release of *RoboCop* on Laserdisc and DVD came at a time when Verhoeven's American career was coming to an end; *Hollow Man* (2000) would be Verhoeven's final Hollywood film before he voluntarily repatriated to Europe. Due to licensing rights the Criterion release of *RoboCop* on DVD is now out of print and will remain so until one day Criterion or another boutique label release the film again on the Blu-ray format, which certainly would be a welcome sight indeed for fans of the film.

While *RoboCop* was given the Criterion treatment, the film is also considered a significant moment in the evolution of director Paul Verhoeven, the transition from Europe to Hollywood finally coming to a creative fruition, which for a while looked in doubt.

Furthermore, the involvement of Orion Pictures is another factor that is often overlooked in the story of *RoboCop*. Orion had enjoyed a previous unexpected success with *The Terminator*, shot on a low budget and directed by James Cameron, and so understood better than anyone how to market a cyborg science fiction. It is unlikely that a major studio would have wanted to back a project like *RoboCop* given its edgy script. In the late 1980 and early 1990s, Orion had a great critical and commercial run of films including *Amadeus* (1984), *Platoon* (1986), *Dances With Wolves* (1990) and *The Silence of the Lambs* (1991). The idea of 'quality Hollywood' became associated with Orion but it was short lived. The overheads of trying to compete with the major Hollywood studios coupled with the commercial under-performance of too many films meant that in the early 1990s Orion faced bankruptcy, although it kept going well into the late 1990s. In many ways, Orion found a niche, supporting the auteur director and taking a risk on difficult film projects, which major studios saw as a commercial liability. In this respect *RoboCop* is not even a Hollywood film as it was effectively made outside of the normal studio infrastructure. Perhaps this institutional variance is what made *RoboCop* such a decidedly recalcitrant work, one that could indubitably accommodate the nonconformist sentiments of Paul Verhoeven.

Marketing *RoboCop*

In the summer of 1987 *RoboCop* was an unexpected sleeper hit but Orion started to market the film very early, learning from the positive experience of *The Terminator*. In a piece written for the Los Angeles Times titled 'The Marketing of a Mechanical Hero', Jack Mathews maps out some of the key reasons for the film's commercial success starting with early press screenings which Orion banked on because of the critical reputation of Paul Verhoeven. The early critical reaction was favourable, boding well for the film's release. Charles Glenn, Head of Marketing for Orion, used a number of novel strategies to promote awareness about the film's release including: 'Models and actors wearing fiberglass replicas of *RoboCop* costumes began appearing in major cities throughout the United States and Canada three weeks before the opening' (Mathews, 1987: 10). The merchandising opportunities with a comic book fantasy figure like RoboCop was another aspect of the film's marketing that Orion were quick to develop including a Marvel Comics publication, a video game and the requisite novelisation of the film. The film's identity was constructed and articulated through both the poster and trailers for the film, which are aspects of the marketing campaign that I will briefly explore next.

The poster to the film, artwork by Mike Bryan, used the tagline of 'Part Man, Part Machine, All Cop' positioned next to the shiny metallic image of RoboCop in a heroically posed shot that sees him stepping in/out of a Detroit police patrol car. The names of stars are not posited as a selling point, and neither is the director. And like many blockbusters of the 1980s, it is the *concept* of RoboCop that is pitched to audiences. Another prominent feature of the poster is the extenuation of Rob Bottin's elegantly designed RoboCop suit, a major iconographic signifier of the cyborg. The colour scheme made up of muted greys, neon purple and shiny silver creates a specifically dystopian tone while the red from the police siren across the top half of RoboCop's armour connotes an ambiguity about the character. If science fiction is clearly communicative, the genre of neo noir is also current in the use of colours, perhaps suggesting the film was being positioned to appeal to an older, more sophisticated audience. Certainly, for an alleged exploitation film the poster has a simplicity and elegance to it, which explains the continuing popular appeal of the poster.

Unlike the charm of the poster, the original 1987 trailer for *RoboCop* deploys *The Terminator* theme to uneasy effect. And the trailer does make *RoboCop* feel like an exploitation film, mainly because of the tawdry edits. Given the tremendous runaway success of *The Terminator*, Orion naturally transposed the iconic music into the trailer as both a point of familiarity for audiences and in fear of the film failing at the box office. The repeated emphasis in the trailer is the action element of the film, with the gas station explosion providing the background to the end of the trailer. In this context, the marketing of film was geared to audiences and fans of the 1980s hard body action cinema epitomised by Stallone and Schwarzenegger.

Although *RoboCop* was an 18 in the UK and an R in the US, a generation of kids including myself first came upon *RoboCop* on VHS, and in many ways the appeal of RoboCop to a teenager was not just the cyborg identity but the strangely magical quality Hollywood fantasies of this nature could broadly conjure to entertain the imaginations of the youth. In other words, the poster and trailer told us that RoboCop was cool. Maybe in today's age of sanitised comic book superheroes in which we rarely if ever witness the impact of violence and see any of the blood and bits that come out of people when they get shot, *RoboCop* represents a bygone age of pre-internet Hollywood cinema.

The Sequels: *RoboCop* as a Franchise

I next want to focus on the sequels, *RoboCop 2* (1990) and *RoboCop 3* (1993), which together with the first film form a loose trilogy. Both of these films were made to capitalise on the success of the first film, setting in motion a franchise, which became unsustainable given the dwindling box office returns. However, in 2014 *RoboCop* was given a re-boot, again with the intent of re-establishing a potential franchise. The brilliance of the first film was never replicated and much of this can be attributed to the direction of Paul Verhoeven who would leave an indelible mark on the Hollywood science fiction genre. But it is still worth considering the relationship between the original film and the two sequels.

RoboCop 2 was rushed into production with the hope of cashing in on the success of the first film. While producer Jon Davison and actor Peter Weller returned, much of the original crew did not, notably Paul Verhoeven and the original writers. *RoboCop 2* is an inferior film, marred by a pedestrian direction and an uninspiring script. However, corporate power and the War on Drugs are two themes still resonate. We are informed by the media break that OCP is still in conflict with the police, cutting salaries. Unlike the first film where the Old Man is somewhat peripheral and benign, in *RoboCop 2* he is depicted as far more insidious and ruthless. Anticipating the city of Detroit will default on loan payments, the Old Man informs the Mayor of Detroit that once foreclosure begins OCP will have the legality to take over the assets of the city: 'We're taking Detroit private', exclaims the Old Man. When challenged by the Mayor for his unscrupulous corporate pathology, the Old Man retorts: 'Anyone can buy OCP stock and own a piece of the city. What can be more democratic than that?' The privatisation of Detroit is made altogether more explicit in the second film but the political drama lacks the presence of a Dick Jones or Clarence Boddicker to make the Machiavellian intrigue workable. A second continuing theme is the War on Drugs that was still current throughout the early 1990s. 'NUKE', an aptly titled narcotic that has Detroit in a spiral of addiction, is a plague of crack cocaine that has infiltrated inner city America. In the first film, the problem of drug addiction is very much a social problem that exists in the backdrop but in *RoboCop 2* the proliferation of drug abuse impacts the strata of American society that includes the police, which may seem a little far fetched. And NUKE is depicted as more than just a drug but a cult movement led by Cain, another white sociopath with delusions of Messianic rapture, played by the imposing character actor Tom Noonan.

In 1993, Orion released *RoboCop 3*. It was a film that had been shot in 1991 but the release was delayed due to Orion filing for bankruptcy. While *RoboCop 3* is technically an inferior film, compared to its predecessors, the corporate politics are in fact slightly more socialist. It was directed by Fred Dekker and saw Robert Burke replacing Peter Weller as Murphy/RoboCop. Like *RoboCop 2*, the screenplay was by comic writer Frank Miller. *RoboCop 3* opens with the familiar media break news report, informing us that OCP has been taken over by a Japanese conglomerate, a trend in corporate America that had started in the 1980s. Yet another crime wave has hit Detroit, a tired narrative situation by now, but this time we find a resistance group made up of homeless, ordinary citizens standing up to the corporate might of OCP.

In *RoboCop 3*, the demolition of Old Detroit has become a nightmarish truth. In the opening sequence, a family is served an eviction notice and then rousted out of their home when a wrecking ball comes crashing through the bedroom window. The displacement of working class populations so that they can make way for new shopping malls and middle class urban development is enabled through gentrification practiced by corporations like OCP. OCP have initiated a group of rehabilitation officers whose job is to 'cleanse' the neighbourhoods, and while the figure of RoboCop becomes displaced somewhat from the class politics of the narrative, the film goes a long way to recapturing some of the anarchic energy of the first film. Nonetheless, *RoboCop 3* is devoid of the graphic violence the first two films had worked to establish as a defining characteristic of the franchise's grubby, trash aesthetic. However, there is a political dissent in *RoboCop 3*, which finally pits the masses against the oppressive corporation in a crude street battle at the end of the film. This is where we also for the first time in the series find RoboCop align himself politically in direct opposition to the corporation for which he has functioned as a hegemonic extension. Dissent leads to open revolt. One of the newscasters on media break refuses to read a news item branding RoboCop as a terrorist, walking off set live on air. Soon, the Detroit police revolt against OCP, improbably so, joining the resistance. If all of this sounds a tad far fetched, it is. Besides this ideological rhetoric, *RoboCop 3* has perhaps the weakest narrative arc of the three films and descends into a farcical parody with moments of outright silliness like the taming of ED-209 into an obedient puppy!

Verhoeven and Science Fiction

The success of *RoboCop* led to an interest in science fiction cinema that would lead Paul Verhoeven to direct three more science fiction films; *Total Recall*, *Starship Troopers* and *Hollow Man*. None of the films are pure science fiction but hybrids, fusing conventions from a broad range of genres including war movie, horror and the political thriller. Verhoeven also directed *Basic Instinct* (1992) and *Showgirls* (1995), both riotously underrated Hollywood films in their own way.[36]

Total Recall, a star vehicle for Arnold Schwarzenegger and based on a short story by famed science fiction writer Philip K Dick, was a big budget science fiction spectacular aimed at the summer crowd. *Total Recall* like *RoboCop* is about memories, identity and the corporation. But unlike the future visual design of *RoboCop*, which is of the now, *Total Recall*'s setting on Mars is a projection about the future. Satire is less evident; difficult to do when the film is stuffed full of brilliantly executed action set pieces, proving what Verhoeven was capable of with a bigger budget. The goal of protagonist Doug Quaid, played by Schwarzenegger in a mildly engaging performance, is to ultimately liberate the oppressed people of Mars – he becomes an inadvertent saviour just like RoboCop but there is an inherent lack of political subtext in the ideological address. Also gone is the complicated satirical bite of *RoboCop*, instead replaced by an overabundance of visual effects. The more I watch *Total Recall*, the less affection I have for it. Nonetheless, what *Total Recall* really does well is live up to the claim of being a solid summer blockbuster film, a difficult feat.

Verhoeven returned to science fiction after seven years, directing *Starship Troopers*, an adaptation of Robert Heinlein's 1959 right-wing novel, and reteaming with much of the crew from *RoboCop* and *Total Recall*, including with *RoboCop* writer Ed Neumeier and producer Jon Davison. Unlike *Total Recall*, which is overrated today, *Starship Troopers* received a lukewarm response from critics in 1997. But, in many respects *Starship Troopers* is the film that continues to grow in critical estimation, and it is Verhoeven's sharpest and most political Hollywood work, a film as subversive as *RoboCop* in its satirical bent.

Starship Troopers begins like *RoboCop* but with a markedly futuristic media break. Roz Kaveney says 'Verhoeven used a somewhat similar device in *RoboCop*, where the narrative is interspersed with chunks of media-surfing from which we assemble a picture of *RoboCop*'s world' (Kaveney, 2005: 19). Gone are the newscasters, replaced by an innocuous voice-over that guides the viewer through what is a perpetual barrage of propaganda. A military recruitment advert, aimed at persuading the youth to join the fight against colonising arachnids is even more on the nose in terms of satire than any of the ads seen in *RoboCop*. The film's subversive tone is set up immediately, one in which a future society promotes war as a fun pastime, making it more than just palatable but one absurdly and undemocratically quarantying citizenship. The recruitment ad is followed by the transmission of the live invasion of a planet in which we find a reporter embedded as part of the army, later to be a key feature of the media's wholly biased coverage of the War in Iraq, only to be eaten alive on air by a giant bug which goes about severing the poor reporter's body in two. It is a moment of dark humour that recalls the comical carnage of Kinney's obliteration by ED-209 in *RoboCop*. If the arachnids exemplify the inevitability historical force of colonialisation then it is a mutual theme bringing together Verhoeven's science fiction trilogy. There is a deliberate artificiality to *Starship Troopers* brilliantly realised in the overall design of the film from the teen caricatures (inspired casting) to the set-piece situations culled from famous alien invasion films. Even more on the nose is the politics of the film, a hilariously discursive exploration of fascism[37] with Verhoeven and Neumeier bringing to fruition themes that were merely lurking beneath the surface of *RoboCop*.

Verhoeven's last American film to-date and final science fiction genre piece was *Hollow Man*, an interpretation of The Invisible Man story. Read as an allegory for contemporary body politics, the parallels with *RoboCop* are striking from this particular perspective since both films deal with one man's attempts to regain control over a body, a struggle for spectral recognition. Probably the least seen of Verhoeven's American films, *Hollow Man* is arguably worth a closer look today.

Afterword: Be Kind, Don't Rewind

Following the critical and commercial failure of *Hollow Man*, Verhoeven moved back to Europe. After a hiatus of six years Verhoeven returned in 2006 with the superb Dutch World War II thriller *Black Book*, a work that reiterated Verhoeven's significance as an international filmmaker. In 2016, Verhoeven's most recent film *Elle*, starring Isabelle Hupert, dealing with the politics of rape, premiered enthusiastically at the Cannes Film Festival. It is unlikely Verhoeven will return to Hollywood but after nearly thirty years, *RoboCop* is still one of his richest works.

Michel Gondry's homage to *RoboCop* in *Be Kind Rewind* (2008), a film that is 'sweded' – a term referring to popular films innovatively re-enacted using a camcorder with the most perfunctory of budgets, reiterated the continuing fondness with which *RoboCop* has become part of popular culture. Gondry's inclusion of *RoboCop* as part of nostalgia for VHS, old media, as something retro is part of a cultural flow in which cinematic memories were forged in a discordant pattern of adolescent subterfuge and waiting impatiently at the video store for the tape to arrive with the hope it hasn't been chewed up by someone else's VCR. Perhaps the epitome of *RoboCop*'s cultural popularity was the release of a crowd-funded project, 'Our *RoboCop* Remake', in 2014. Fifty filmmakers worked together to re-tell the story of *RoboCop* in a celebratory pastiche. Most recently, a comprehensive documentary on the making of *RoboCop*, 'RoboDoc: The creation of *RoboCop*' (2017), once again reiterates the many ways in which the film continues to capture the imagination.

With the endlessly banal culture of rebooting film franchises, *RoboCop* was finally re-made in 2014 with a hefty budget and swish marketing campaign.[38] Unfortunately, due to my unapologetic adoration for the films I have grown up with and contempt I have for contemporary Hollywood salivating to cash in on anything that could be re-hashed as a potential new franchise I have no desire to see the latest *RoboCop* re-incarnation. Ever. Undoubtedly, though, there have been great science fiction films in recent years, notably *Children of Men* (2009) and *Under the Skin* (2013), both of which have a radical political address.

Thankfully, after all these years, *RoboCop* continues to endure. I return to the film on a regular basis and find it speaking to me in new and different ways – politically, stylistically and theologically. But I guess why it really grabbed me when I saw it for the first time in my youth was to do with the identity crisis faced by RoboCop/Murphy. As a British Asian who went to a predominately white school and who was also going through his own personal identity crisis at the time, I related to and understood the gaze of the outsider, the ghostly yet empathetic man-machine looking at the world and trying desperately to figure out his place in the universe. And for a brief while, *RoboCop* let me see the stars.

Footnotes

1. This point about silly film titles may seem a little inconsequential given the age in which we are living in is fundamentally populated by an endless canon of ridiculously titled films that have been successful with audiences. But then *RoboCop* does sound like a cheap exploitation flick, and perhaps that was the real intention.

2. *The Terminator* is still widely regarded as James Cameron's best film and may just be the greatest B movie ever made.

3. For other notorious examples of BBC dubbing, please see B*everly Hills Cop, Midnight Run* and every other 1980s Eddie Murphy film. Another famous dubbing incident that I could never quite get over was in ITV's *Ghostbusters* broadcast, which resulted in replacing the evergreen Bill Murray line 'This man has no dick' with 'This man has no Twinkie'.

4. The video nasty scare of the 1980s led to some films being banned by the BBFC if they had not been classified. Video nasties was fuelled the hysteria of a right wing media and coincided with the advent of Video Cassette Recorders (VCRs).

5. *The Man in the Iron Mask* (1850) by Alexander Dumas is another distant influence on both the Iron Man films and *RoboCop*.

6. More than ever the dreaded term auteur polarises critics and audiences but the idea of authorship for directors work labelled as trash or exploitation can often help in the process of reclaiming their films. However, in the field of reception studies authorship is simply one context in which a director's work can be reclaimed from the past. But the auteur theory has often been explored in relation to genre studies, and it is the tensions between the two that have proven to be instructive but in no way definitive.

7. Director Monte Hellman shot second unit in Dallas including 'RoboCop going through his old house'.

8. Basil Poledouris is often overlooked in the pantheon of Hollywood film composers, having produced some very memorable scores including *Conan The Barbarian* and *The Hunt for Red October*.

9. In Hindu culture the soul is referred to as the 'Atman', the eternal self, and in many ways, RoboCop's quest to reclaim his true self is akin to Eastern philosophical beliefs.

10. There have never been pure genres, so hybridity is an old concept. Most films have always drawn on the repertoire of elements from many different genres, engaging in a practice of fusion, exchange and bricolage.

11. Neill Blomkamp's *Elysium* (2013) is a science fiction film that returns to the theme of the oppressed worker drone while the white saviour protagonist chimes with that of *RoboCop*.

12. Much of the film was shot in Dallas in 1986 and made extensive use of the city's urban landscapes.

13. Tag Gallagher says using John Ford's work to trace the evolution of the Western makes for the 'worst possible paradigm' since the 'cyclical alternations in Ford's vision and style occur regardless of the genre in which he is working' (Gallager, 1986: 257).

14. ED-209 was designed by visual effects artist Craig Davies and animated by the legendary Phil Tippett.

15. *Heaven's Gate* (1980) was notoriously ignored for many years because of the financial crisis the film posed for United Artists. Thankfully, *Heaven's Gate* has been reclaimed and stands as one of the great Westerns of the contemporary era.

16. Robert DoQui (1934 – 2008) was a character actor who started out in television in the early 1960s, slowly graduating to film.

17. Peter Weller had yet to break through in Hollywood. The closest he had come to stardom was with the cult film *The Adventures of the Buckaroo Banzai Across the 8th Dimension* (1984). Weller has a Doctorate in Italian Renaissance Art History from UCLA (2014).

18. Bonding between men and women occurs regularly in the Hawks universe, prominently through the exchange of cigarettes. The Western films of Hawks include *Red River, Rio Bravo*, and *El Dorado*.

19. This line has seeped into movie folklore but its intertextual resonance goes back to the mythology of the American cowboy, both historically and culturally.

20. Many classic Westerns notably the films of Sergio Leone use children as an ideological construct and are often shown to be the victims of violence.

21. The Tatooine massacre of Aunt Beru and Owen Lars by imperial storm troopers at the behest of Darth Vader in *A New Hope* vividly recalls the moment in *The Searchers* when Ethan returns to the homestead to find the farm ablaze and his extended family dead.

22. There are many types of repression that Wood lists including sexual energy, bisexuality, severe repression of female sexuality/creativity and repression of the sexuality of children.

23. In his analysis Barry Grant focuses on film such as *After Hours* (1985), *Something Wild* (1986), *Fatal Attraction* (1987), *Bad Influence* (1991) and *Single White Female* (1992).

24. In the director's cut of the film this sequence runs a minute longer, including graphic imagery that was trimmed back for the original 1987 release.

25. Reading *RoboCop* as a comic book fantasy would imply this particular montage of heroism is typically signposted in comic book cinema when the comic book hero shows off his skills in a celebratory spectacle.

26. I'm increasingly convinced *Metropolis* is one of the few films that form the centre of the cinematic universe.

27. Thomas Byers uses *Blade Runner* along with *Alien* and *Star Trek 2* to 'explore the relationship between high tech corporate capitalism...and individual modes and styles of personal behaviour on the other' (Byers, 1987: 39).

28. Neumeier's recollection evokes the corporate disobedience of *Fight Club*'s worker drone, another strident capitalist satire from a Hollywood studio.

29. Media break would become a prevailing thematic motif and narrative device in the later *RoboCop* films and is one I look at briefly in the final chapter.

30. Perestroika (means restructuring) was Gorbachev's reform of the Soviet Union, which meant modernisation, and a new political dialogue of openness with the West.

31. 'Icky' is the expression writer Neumeier uses in the Criterion DVD commentary to describe Clarence Boddicker since he spits on everything.

32. One only needs to be reminded of the controversy surrounding Scorsese's *The Last Temptation of Christ* (1988), another re-telling of Jesus's story but from a plural, secularist and contemporary perspective. The Catholic Church and Christian fundamentalist groups opposed the release of the film vehemently. This almost led to Universal backing down and completely suppressing the film.

33. The Jesus Seminar was made up of a large body of respected scholars who pursued a long-term academic goal of reconstructing the historical life of Jesus Christ.

34. Paul Verhoeven has a Doctorate in Mathematics and Psychics, which certainly qualifies him as a learned scholar and academic.

35. The OCP prime directives that RoboCop must adhere to are based on Isaac Azimov's three laws of robotics: 1). A robot may not injure a human being or, through inaction, allow a human being to come to harm, 2). A robot must obey the orders given it by human beings, except where such orders would conflict with the First Law, 3). A robot must protect its own existence as long as such protection does not conflict with the First or Second Laws.

36. For a terrific defence and critique read the wonderful monograph by film critic Adam Nayman, *It Doesn't Suck: Showgirls* (2014).

37. For a more detailed reading of the relationship between Heinlein's novel and the film see Chapter 3 'Director as Parodist: Paul Verhoeven's *Starship Troopers*' of *From Alien to the Matrix: Reading Science Fiction Film* (Roz Kaveney, 2005).

38. Had the re-boot of *RoboCop* remained with Darren Aronofksy and Michael Fassbender then it may have potentially persuaded me to get onboard with the whole enterprise.

Bibliography and Filmography

Books and Journals

Abbott, Joe (1994) 'They Came From Beyond the Center: Ideology and Political Textuality in the Radical Science Fiction Films of James Cameron', *Literature/Film Quarterly*, Jan 1 1994, 22: 1.

Bakan, Joel (2004) *The Corporation: The Pathological Pursuit of Profit and Power*. New York: Free Press.

Bazin, Andre (1955/1971) 'The Evolution of the Western', in *What is Cinema?* vol. 2, trans. by Hugh Gray. Berkeley/Los Angeles/London: University of California Press, pp. 149 – 157.

Bellour, Raymond (1993) *Le Western: Approaches, mythologies, auteurs-acteurs, filmographies*. Paris: Gallimard.

Berman, Russell (1985) 'Rambo: From Counter-Culture to Contra', *Telos* 64, pp. 143 – 147.

Best, Steven (1989) 'RoboCop: In the detritus of hi-technology', *Jump Cut: A Review of Contemporary Media*, No. 34, March 1989, pp. 19 – 26 http://www.ejumpcut.org/archive/onlinessays/JC34folder/RoboCopBest.html (last accessed Friday 22 July 2016).

Best, Steven (1989) 'RoboCop: The Crisis of Subjectivity', *Illuminations* http://www.uta.edu/huma/illuminations/best1.htm (last accessed Friday 22 July 2016).

Booker, M. Keith (2006) *Alternate Americas: Science Fiction Film and American Culture*. Westport, Connecticut/London: Praeger.

Bulhan, Hussein Abdilahi (1985) *Frantz Fanon and the Psychology of Oppression*. New York: Plenum Press.

Campbell, Neil (2013) *Post-westerns: Cinema, region, West*, Lincoln: University of Nebraska Press.

Carter, Matthew (2014) *Myth of the Western*. Edinburgh: Edinburgh University Press.

Cavallaro, Dani (2000) *Cyberpunk and Cyberculture: Science fiction and the work of William Gibson*. London: The Athlone Press.

Cawelti, John (1972) *The Six-Gun Mystique*. Ohio: Bowling Green University Popular Press.

Cawelti, John (1975) 'Myths of Violence in American Popular Culture', *Critical Inquiry*, Vol. 1, No. 3 (March), pp. 521-542.

Cawelti, John (1985) 'The Questions of Popular Genres', *Journal of Popular Film and Television*, Vol. 13, No. 2 (Summer) pp. 55-61.

Codell, Julie F. (1989) 'RoboCop: Murphy's Law, RoboCop's body, and capitalism's work', *Jump Cut: A Review of Contemporary Media*, No. 34, March 1989, pp. 12 – 19.

Cornea, Christine (2007) *Science Fiction Cinema: Between Fantasy and Reality*. Edinburgh: Edinburgh University Press.

Ebert, Roger (1987) RoboCop Film Review, *Chicago Sun-Times* http://www.rogerebert.com/reviews/RoboCop-1987 (last accessed Friday 22 July 2016).

Everson, William (1969) *A Pictorial History of the Western Film*, Secaucus: Citadel Press.

French, Philip (1977), *Western: Aspects of a movie genre*. Oxford/New York: Oxford University Press.

Frye, Northrop (1957) *Anatomy of Criticism*. Princeton: Princeton University Press.

Gallagher, Tag (1986), 'Shoot-Out at the Genre Corral: Problems in the "Evolution" of the Western' in Grant, Barry Keith (ed.) *Film Genre Reader III*. Austin: University of Texas Press.

Gallardo, Ximena & Smith, Jason (2004) *Alien Woman: The making of Lt. Ellen Ripley*. New York: Continuum.

Grant, Barry (1996) 'Rich and Strange: The Yuppie Horror Film', *Journal of Film and Video*, Vol. 48, No. 1-2 (Spring-Summer), pp. 4-16.

Haraway, Donna (1990; first published 1984), 'A Manifesto for Cyborgs: Science, Technology & Socialist Feminism in the 1980s', in Nicholson, Linda J. (ed.), *Feminism/Postmodernism*. New York/London: Routledge.

Jeffords, Susan (1994) *Hard Bodies: Hollywood masculinity in the Reagan era*. New Brunswick, N.J.: Rutgers University Press.

Kain, Erik (2011) 'Ridley Scott's "Prometheus" and the Science Fiction of Corporatism', *Forbes* http://www.forbes.com/sites/erikkain/2011/12/28/ridley-scotts-prometheus-and-the-science-fiction-of-corporatism/#1dd5a594212d (last accessed Friday 22 July 2016).

Kitses, Jim (1970) *Horizons West: Studies of Authorship within the Western*. Bloomington: Indiana University Press.

Kozlovic, Anton Karl (2004) 'The Cinematic Christ-Figure', *The Furrow*, Vol. 55, No. 1, pp. 26 – 30.

Kozlovic, Anton Karl (2001) 'From Holy Aliens to Cyborg Saviours: Biblical Subtexts in Four Science Fiction Films', *Journal of Religion and Film*, Vol. 5, No. 2.

Kuenz, Jane (2001) 'The Cowboy Businessman and The Course of Empire: Owen Wister's The Virginian', *Cultural Critique*, No. 48 (Spring), pp. 98-128.

Malone, Peter (2012) *Screen Jesus: Portrayals of Christ in television and film*. Lanham: Scarecrow Press.

Manaugh, Geoff (2014) 'The Original RoboCop was a Christ Allegory', Gizmodo http://gizmodo.com/the-original-RoboCop-was-a-christ-allegory-1523956164 (last accessed Friday 22 July 2016).

Melehy, Hasaan (2004) 'Bodies Without Organs: Cyborg Cinema of the 1980s', in Rickman, Gregg (ed.), *The Science Fiction Film Reader*. New York: Limelight.

Nama, Adilifu (2008) *Black Space: Imagining race in science fiction film*. Austin: University of Texas Press.

Napier, Susan J. (2004) 'Ghosts and Machines: The Technological Body', in Redmond, Sean (ed.), *Liquid Metal: The science fiction film reader*. London/New York: Wallflower Press.

Neale, Steve (2000), *Genre and Hollywood*. London: Routledge.

Nachbar, Jack (1974), *Focus on the Western*. Englewoods Cliffs: Prentice-Hall.

Newton, Judith (1990), 'Feminism and Anxiety in Alien', in Kuhn, Annette (ed.), *Alien Zone: Cultural Theory and Contemporary Science Fiction Cinema*. London/New York: Verso.

Petley, Julian (1988) 'Flemish and Fantastic: An interview with Paul Verhoeven', *Monthly Film Bulletin*; Feb 1.

Pye, Douglas (1975) 'Genre and Movies', *Movie*, 20: 29-43.

Redmond, Sean (ed.) (2004) *Liquid Metal: The science fiction film reader*. London/New York: Wallflower Press.

Reinhartz, Adele (2013) *Bible and Cinema: An Introduction*. London/New York: Routledge.

Roth, Lane (1985) 'Vraisemblance and the Western Setting in Contemporary Science Fiction Film', *Literature/Film Quarterly*, Jan 1, Vol. 13, No. 3.

Ryan, Michael & Kellner, Douglas (1988) *Camera Politica: The Politics and Ideology of Contemporary Hollywood film*. Bloomington: Indiana University Press.

Schaub, Joseph Christopher (2001) 'Kusanagi's Body: Gender and Technology in Mecha-anime', *Asian Journal of Communication*, Vol. 11, No. 22.

Schatz, Thomas (1981) *Hollywood Genres: formulas, filmmaking, and the studio system*. New York: Random House.

Schrader, Paul (2010) 'In Development' (Book review of Verhoeven's *Jesus of Nazareth*), *Film Comment*, July-August.

Seed, David (2011) *Science Fiction: A very short introduction*. Oxford/New York: Oxford University Press.

Simmon, Scott (2003) *The Invention of the Western Film: A cultural history of the genre's first half century*. Cambridge/New York: Cambridge University Press.

Smelik, Anneke (2010) *The Scientific Imaginary in Visual Culture*. Goettingen: V&R unipress.

Sobchack, Vivian (1997) *Screening Space: The American Fiction Film*. New Brunswick/New Jersey/London: Rutgers University Press.

Sontag, Susan (1994) A*gainst Interpretation*. London: Vintage.

Springer, Claudia (1996) *Electronic Eros: Bodies and Desire in the Postindustrial Age*. London: The Athlone Press.

Telotte, J.P. (1994) 'In the Realm of Revealing: The Technological Double in Contemporary Science Fiction Film', *Journal of the Fantastic in the Arts*, Vol. 6, No. 2/3, pp. 234-252.

Van Scheers, Rob (1997) *Paul Verhoeven*. London/Boston: Faber.

Verhoeven, Paul (2010) *Jesus of Nazareth*. New York: Seven Stories Press.

Warshow, Robert (1962) *The Immediate Experience: Movie, Comics, Theatre and Other Aspects of Popular Culture*. Garden City, N.Y.: Doubleday.

Wood, Robin (1986) *Hollywood from Vietnam to Reagan*. New York: Columbia University Press.

Wright, Will (1975) *Six Guns and Society: A structural study of the Western*. Berkeley: University of California Press.

Newspapers and Magazines

Denby, David. 'The Soul of a Blue Machine.' *Time*. July 27, 1987.

Ebert, Roger. *New York Post*. July 17, 1987.

French, Sean. *Monthly Film Bulletin*. Winter 1988.

Goodman, Walter. *New York Times*. July 17, 1987.

Kael, Pauline. *New Yorker*. August 8, 1987.

Kehr, Dave. *Chicago Tribune*. July 17, 1987.

Mantel, Hilary. 'Good clean violence.' *The Spectator*. February 20, 1988.

Mathews, Jack. 'The Marketing of a Mechanical Hero.' *LA Times*. July 21, 1987.

Salamon, Julie. *Wall Street Journal*. July 23, 1987.

Sterritt, David. *Christian Science Monitor*. August 7, 1987.

Strick, Phillip. *Monthly Film Bulletin*. February 1985.

Williamson, Judith. *New Statesman*. February 19, 1988.

Wilmington, Michael. 'High Marks for High Tech.' *LA Times*. July 17, 1987.

Filmography

The Adventures of the Buckaroo Banzai Across the 8th Dimension (1984)

After Hours (1985)

Alien (1979)

Alien 3 (1992)

Aliens (1986)

All the Presidents Men (1976)

Avatar (2009)

Bad Influence (1991)

Back to the Future Part III (1990)

Basic Instinct (1992)

Be Kind Rewind (2008)

Beverly Hills Cop (1984)

Blade Runner (1982)

Chappie (2015)

Children of Men (2009)

Close Encounters of the Third Kind (1977)

Conan the Barbarian (1982)

The Conversation (1974)

Cowboys and Aliens (2011)

The Day the Earth Stood Still (1951)

El Dorado (1967)

Elysium (2013)

E.T. (1982)

Fatal Attraction (1987)

Fight Club (1999)

Flesh & Blood (1985)

The Godfather (1974)

Heaven's Gate (1980)

High Noon (1952)

The Hunt for Red October (1990)

The Iron Giant (1999)

Iron Man (2008)

John Carter (2012)

Klute (1971)

The Last Temptation of Christ (1988)

The Matrix (1999)

Metropolis (1927)

Midnight Run (1988)

Night Moves (1975)

Once Upon a Time in the West (1968)

Outland (1981)

The Ox-Bow Incident (1943)

The Parallax View (1974)

Predator (1987)

Prometheus (2012)

Pursued (1947)

RoboCop 2 (1990)

RoboCop 3 (1993)

Rollerball (1978)

Rambo First Blood: Part II (1985)

Ramrod (1947)

Red River (1948)

Rio Bravo (1959)

The Searchers (1956)

Shane (1953)

Showgirls (1995)

Single White Female (1992)

Something Wild (1986)

Star Wars: A New Hope (1977)

Starman (1984)

Starship Troopers (1997)

The Terminator (1984)

Terminator 2: Judgment Day (1992)

They Live (1988)

Total Recall (1990)

Under the Skin (2013)

Westworld (1973)

The Wild Bunch (1969)

Wild Wild West (1999)

CONSTELLATIONS
studies in science fiction film and TV

CLOSE ENCOUNTERS OF THE THIRD KIND

Jon Towlson

CONSTELLATIONS
studies in science fiction film and TV

INCEPTION

David Carter